*March of America Facsimile Series*

*Number 15*

# Thomas Hariot's Virginia

Theodore de Bry

# Thomas Hariot's Virginia

*by Theodore de Bry*

**ANN ARBOR**

**UNIVERSITY MICROFILMS, INC.**

*A Subsidiary of Xerox Corporation*

56776

Thomas Hariot's Virginia

# Foreword

When Sir Walter Raleigh sent his colonists to Roanoke Island in 1585 he included in the group a scientist, Thomas Hariot (also spelled Harriot), and an artist, John White. On their return to England, Hariot published *A briefe and true report of the new found land of Virginia* (1588). White brought back beautiful watercolor drawings of plant, animal, and human life in Virginia. Soon after the publication of Hariot's book, a German engraver and publisher, Theodore de Bry of Frankfurt, was in London and made the acquaintance of Richard Hakluyt, Hariot, and White. An agreement was reached for the publication of Hariot's book, illustrated with engravings based on White's drawings. De Bry brought the volume out at Frankfurt in 1590 in four languages, Latin, French, German, and English, which gave Hariot's and White's work on the New World a wide circulation in Europe. A second edition in Latin and German appeared in 1608. The English version of 1590 is reproduced here. The four versions appear as Part I of de Bry's America.

Although Hariot's account served as propaganda for Raleigh's efforts to establish a colony in the New World, it is a careful report of the observations of a man with scientific interests and is one of the most valuable of the early descriptions of North America. White's magnificent drawings, slightly altered in de Bry's engravings, provide a visual representation of what a trained artist saw. The probability is that Richard Hakluyt, the great advocate of colonial expansion, brought this material to de Bry's attention.

Since de Bry was a German, working at Frankfurt with German printers, the diction and spelling of his own preface and some of the notes to the pictures are sometimes bizarre.

The notes for the engraved pictures were written in Latin by Thomas Hariot and translated into English by Richard Hakluyt, though de Bry and his German colleagues seem to have taken a hand in the notes, not always to their improvement. A map of the region discussed by Hariot was also included.

Curiously, de Bry added to the volume some engravings of Picts, ancient inhabitants of Britain, which White had made and which de Bry noticed among his drawings. White's imaginary pictures of the Picts were taken, he claimed, from an old chronicle.

White provided de Bry with a set of his drawings, which he took back to his workshop in Frankfurt. The ultimate fate of these drawings is not known; they are not identical with those preserved in the British Museum but apparently were copies.

The best discussion of the White drawings, and of Hariot's connection with de Bry's enterprise, is to be found in *The American Drawings of John White, 1557-1590* by Paul Hulton and David B. Quinn (London and Chapel Hill, N. C., 1964), I, 25-27. A facsimile reproduction of Hariot's *A briefe and true report of the new found land of Virginia* (1588), brought out by Edwards Brothers (Ann Arbor, Michigan, 1931), has a useful bibliographical discussion of the original edition by Randolph G. Adams. Information on de Bry will be found in Michael Bryan's, *Dictionary of Painters and Engravers* (London, 1926-1930).

A briefe and true report of the new found land of Virginia, of the commodities and of the nature and manners of the naturall inhabitants. Discouered by the English Colony there seated by Sir Richard Greinuile Knight In the yeere 1585. Which Remained Vnder the gouernement of twelue monethes, At the speciall charge and direction of the Honourable SIR WALTER RALEIGH Knight lord Warden of the stanneries Who therein hath beene fauoured and authorised by her MAIESTIE and her letters patents: This fore booke Is made in English By Thomas Hariot seruant to the abouenamed Sir WALTER, a member of the Colony, and there imployed in discouering

CVM GRATIA ET PRIVILEGIO CÆS. MA.TIS SPECIA.LI

FRANCOFORTI AD MOENVM
TYPIS IOANNIS WECHELI, SVMTIBVS VERO THEODORI
DE BRY ANNO CIↃ IↃ XC.
VENALES REPERIVNTVR IN OFFICINA SIGISMVNDI FEIRABENDII

Pictoon a winp.                    Theodore de Brij fe.

# TO THE RIGHT
## WORTHIE AND HONOV-
### RABLE, SIR VVALTER RALEGH,
KNIGHT, SENESCHAL OF THE DVCHIES OF
Cornewall and Exeter, and L. Warden of the stannaries in Deuon
and Cornewall. T.B. wisheth true felictie.

AMORE ET VIRTVTE,

*IR, seeing that the parte of the Worlde, which is betwene the*
*FLORIDA and the Cap BRETON nowe nammed UIRGI-*
*NIA, to the honneur of yours most souueraine Layde and Quee-*
*ne ELIZABETZ, hath ben descouuerd by yours meanes. And*
*great chardges. And that your Collonye hath been theer estab-*
*lished to your great honnor and prayse, and noe lesser proffit vnto the common*

4

welth: It ys good raison that euery man euertwe him selfe for to showe the bene-
fit which they haue receue of yt. Theerfore, for my parte I haue been allwayes
Desirous for to make yow knowe the good will that I haue to remayne still your
most humble seruant. I haue thincke that I cold faynde noe better occasion to
declare yt, then takinge the paines to cott in copper (the most diligentye and well
that wear in my possible to doe) the Figures which doe leuelye represent the forme aud maner of the Inhabitants of the same countrye with theirs ceremonies,
sollemne, feastes, and the manner and situation of their Townes, or Villages.
Addinge vnto euery figure a brief declaration of the same, to that ende that eue-
rye man cold the better vnderstand that which is in liuelye represented. Moreouer I haue thincke that the aforesaid figures wear of greater commendation, If
somme Histoire which traitinge of the commodites and fertillitye of the said coū-
trye weare Ioyned with the same, therfore haue I serue miselfe of the rapport
which Thomas Hariot hath lattely sett foorth, and haue cause them booth togither to be printed for to dedicated vnto you, as a thinge which by reigtte dooth
allreadye apparteyne vnto you. Therfore doe I creaue that you will accept this
little Booke, and take yt In goode partte. And desiringe that fauor that you will
receue me in the nomber of one of your most humble seruantz, besechinge the
l rd to bles and further you in all yours good doinges and actions, and allso to
preserue, and keepe you allwayes in good helthe. And soe I comitt you vnto
the almyhttie, from Franckfort the first of Apprill 1590.

Your most humble seruant,

THEODORVS de BRY.

# TO THE ADVEN-
## TVRERS, FAVORERS, AND
## VVELVVILLERS OF THE EN-
### TERPRISE FOR THE INHABITTING
and planting in VIRGINIA.

SINCE the first vndertaking by Sir Walter Ralegh to deale in the action of discouering of that Countrey which is now called and known by the name of VIRGINIA; many voyages hauing bin thiter made at sundrie times to his great charge; as first in the yeere 1584. and afterwardes in the yeeres 1585. 1586. and now of late this last yeare of 1587. There haue bin diuers and variable reportes with some slanderous and shamefull speeches bruited abroade by many that returned from thence. Especially of that discouery which was made by the Colony transported by Sir Richard Greinuile in the yeare 1585. being of all the others the most principal and as yet of most effect, the time of their abode in the countrey beeing a whole yeare, when as in the other voyage before they staied but sixe weekes; and the others after were onelie for supply and transportation, nothing more being discouered then had been before. Which reports haue not done a litle wrong to many that otherwise would haue also fauoured & aduentured in the action, to the honour and benefite of our nation, besides the particular profite and credite which would redound to them selues the dealers therein; as I hope by the sequele of euents to the shame of those that haue auouched the contrary shalbe manifest: if you the aduenturers, fauourers, and welwillers do but either encrease in number, or in opinion continue, or hauing bin doubtfull renewe your good liking and furtherance to deale therein according to the worthinesse thereof alreadye found and as you shall vnderstand hereafter to be requisite. Touching which woorthines through cause of the diuersitie of relations and reportes, manye of your opinions coulde not bee firme, nor the mindes of some that are well disposed, bee setled in any certaintie.

I haue therefore thought it good beeing one that haue beene in the discouerie and in dealing with the naturall inhabitantes specially imploied; and hauing therefore seene and knowne more then the ordinarie: to imparte so much vnto you of the fruites of our labours, as that you may knowe howe iniuriously the enterprise is slaundered. And that in publike manner at this present chiefelie for two respectes.

First that some of you which are yet ignorant or doubtfull of the state thereof, may see that there is sufficiét cause why the cheefe enterpriser with the fauour of her Maiestie, notwithstanding suche reportes; hath not onelie since continued the action by sending into the countrey againe, and replanting this last yeere a new Colony; but is also readie, according as the times and meanes will affoorde, to follow and prosecute the same.

Secondly, that you seeing and knowing the continuance of the action by the view hereof you may generally know & learne what the countrey is, & ther vpon côsider how your dealing therein if it proceede, may returne you profit and gaine; bee it either by inhabitting & planting or otherwise in furthering thereof.

And least that the substance of my relation should be doubtful vnto you, as of others by reason of their diuersitie: I will first open the cause in a few wordes wherefore they are ſo different; referring my ſelue to your fauourable conſtructions, and to be adiudged of as by good conſideration you ſhall finde cauſe.

Of our companie that returned ſome for their miſdemenour and ill dealing in the countrey, haue beene there worthily puniſhed; who by reaſon of their badde natures, haue maliciouſly not onelie ſpoken ill of their Gouernours; but for their ſakes ſlaundered the countrie it ſelfe. The like alſo haue thoſe done which were of their conſort.

Some beeing ignorant of the ſtate thereof, notwithſtanding ſince their returne amógeſt their friendes and acquaintance and alſo others, eſpecially if they were in compaine where they might not be gaineſaide; woulde ſeeme to knowe ſo much as no men more; and make no men ſo great trauailers as themſelues. They ſtood ſo much as it maie ſeeme vppon their credite and reputation that hauing been a twelue moneth in the countrey, it woulde haue beene a great diſgrace vnto them as they thought, if they coulde not haue ſaide much wheter it were true or falſe. Of which ſome haue ſpoken of more then euer they ſaw or otherwiſe knew to bee there; otherſome haue not bin aſhamed to make abſolute deniall of that which although not by thē, yet by others is moſt certainely ād there plētifully knowne. And otherſome make difficulties of thoſe things they haue no skill of.

The cauſe of their ignorance was, in that they were of that many that were neuer out of the lland where wee were ſeated, or not farre, or at the leaſtwiſe in few places els, during the time of our aboade in the countrey; or of that many that after golde and ſiluer was not ſo ſoone found, as it was by them looked for, had little or no care of any other thing but to pamper their bellies; or of that many which had little vnderſtanding, leſſe diſcretion, and more tongue then was needfull or requiſite.

Some alſo were of a nice bringing vp, only in cities or townes, or ſuch as neuer (as I may ſay) had ſeene the world before. Becauſe there were not to bee found any Engliſh cities, nor ſuch faire houſes, nor at their owne wiſh any of their olde accuſtomed daintie food, nor any ſoft beds of downe or fethers: the countrey was to them miſerable, & their reports thereof according.

Becauſe my purpoſe was but in briefe to open the cauſe of the varietie of ſuch ſpeeches; the particularities of them, and of many enuious, malicious, and ſlaūderous reports and deuiſes els, by our owne countrey men beſides; as trifles that are not worthy of wiſe men to bee thought vpon, I meane not to trouble you withall: but will paſſe to the commodities, the ſubſtance of that which I haue to make relation of vnto you.

The treatiſe where of for your more readie view & eaſier vnderſtanding I will diuide into three ſpeciall parts. In the firſt I will make declaration of ſuch commodities there alreadie found or to be raiſed, which will not only ſerue the ordinary turnes of you which are and ſhall bee the plāters and inhabitants, but ſuch an ouerplus ſufficiently to bee yelded, or by men of skill to bee prouided, as by way of trafficke and exchaunge with our owne nation of England, will enrich your ſelues the prouiders; thoſe that ſhal deal with you; the enterpriſers in general; and greatly profit our owne countrey men, to ſupply them with moſt things which heretofore they haue bene faine to prouide, either of ſtrangers or of our enemies: which commodities for diſtinction ſake, I call *Merchantable*.

In the ſecond, I will ſet downe all the cōmodities which wee know the countrey by our experience doeth yeld of it ſelfe for victuall, and ſuſtenance of mans life; ſuch as is vſually fed vpon by the inhabitants of the countrey, as alſo by vs during the time we were there.

In the laſt part I will make mention generally of ſuch other cōmodities beſides, as I am able to remember, and as I ſhall thinke behoofull for thoſe that ſhall inhabite, and plant there to knowe of; which ſpecially concerne building, as alſo ſome other neceſſary vſes: with a briefe deſcription of the nature and maners of the people of the countrey.

# To the gentle Reader.

Lthough (frendlye Reader) man by his difobedience, weare depriued of thofe good Gifts wher with he was indued in his creation, yet he was not berefte of wit to prouyde for hym felfe, nor difcretion to deuife things neceffarie for his vfe, except fuche as appartayne to his foules healthe, as may be gathered by this fauage nations, of whome this prefent worke intreateth. For although they haue noe true knoledge of God nor of his holye worde and are deftituted of all lerninge, Yet they paffe vs in many thinges, as in Sober feedinge and Dexteritye of witte, in makinge without any inftrument of mettall thinges fo neate and fo fine, as a man would fcarfelye beleue thefame, Vnless the Englifhemen Had made proofe Therof by their trauailes into the contrye. Confideringe, Therfore that yt was a thinge worthie of admiration, I was verye willinge to offer vnto you the true Pictures of thofe people wich by the helfe of Maifter Richard Hakluyt of Oxford Minifter of Gods Word, who first Incouraged me to publish the Worke, I creaued out of the verye original of Maifter Ihon White an Englifch paynter who was fent into the contrye by the queenes Maieftye, onlye to draw the defcription of the place, lynelye to defcribe the fhapes of the Inhabitants their apparell, manners of Liuinge, and fafhions, att the fpeciall Charges of the worthy knighte, Sir W A L T E R  R A-L E G H, who beftowed noe Small Sume of monnye in the ferche and Difcouerye of that countrye, From te yeers, 1 5 8 4. to the ende of The years 1 5 8 8. Morouer this booke which intreateth of that parte of the new World which the Englifhemen call by the name of Virginia I heer fett out in the firft place, beinge therunto requefted of my Frends, by Raefon of the memorye of the frefh and laue performance ther of, albeyt I haue in hand the Hiftorye of Florida wich fhould bee firft fett foorthe becaufe yt was difcouured by the Frencheman longe befor the difcouerye of Virginia, yet I hope fhortlye alfo to publifh thefame, A Victorye, doubtless fo Rare, as I thinke the like hath not ben heard nor feene. I craeued both of them at London, an brought, Them hither to Franckfurt, wher I and my fonnes hauen taken erneft paynes in grauinge the pictures ther of in Copper, feeing yt is a matter of noe fmall importance. Touchinge the ftile of both the Difcourfes, I haue caufed yt to bee Reduced into verye Good Frenche and Latin by the aide of verye worfhipfull frend of myne. Finallye I hartlye Requeft thee, that yf any feeke to Contrefaict thes my bookx, (for in this dayes many are fo malicious that they feeke to gayne by other men labours) thow wouldeft giue noe credit vnto fuche conterfaited Drawghte. For dyuers fecret marks, e hiddin in my pictures, which wil breede Confufion vnless they bee well obferued.

# THE FIRST PART,
# OF MARCHAN-
## TABLE COMMO-
### DITIES.

*Silke of graſſe or graſſe Silke.*

Here is a kind of graſſe in the countrey vppon the blades where of there groweth very good ſilke in forme of a thin glittering skin to bee ſtript of. It groweth two foote and a halfe high or better: the blades are about two foot in length, and half inch broad. The like groweth in Perſia, which is in the ſelfe ſame climate as Virginia, of which very many of the ſilke workes that come from thence into Europe are made. Here of if it be planted and ordered as in Perſia, it cannot in reaſon be otherwiſe, but that there will riſe in ſhorte time great profite to the dealers therein; ſeeing there is ſo great vſe and vent thereof as well in our countrey as els where. And by the meanes of ſowing & plãting in good ground, it will be farre greater, better, and more plentifull then it is. Although notwithſtanding there is great ſtore thereof in many places of the countrey growing naturally and wilde. Which alſo by proof here in England, in making a piece of ſilke Grogran, we found to be excellent good.

### Worme Silke.

In manie of our iourneyes we found ſilke wormes fayre and great; as bigge as our ordinary walnuttes. Although it hath not beene our happe to haue found ſuch plentic as elſew here to be in the coũtrey we haue heard of; yet ſeeing that the countrey doth naturally breede and nouriſh them, there is no doubt but if art be added in plantig of mulbery trees and others fitte for them in commodious places, for their feeding and nourishing; and some of them carefully gathered and husbanded in that sort as by men of skill is knowne to be necessarie: there will rise as great profite in time to the Virginians, as there of doth now to the Persians, Turkes, Italians and Spaniards.

## Flaxe and Hempe.

The trueth is that of Hempe and Flaxe there is no great store in any one place together, by reason it is not planted but as the soile doth yeeld it of it selfe; and howsoeuer the leafe, and stemme or stalke doe differ from ours; the stuffe by the iudgemét of men of skill is altogether as good as ours. And if not, as further proofe should finde otherwise; we haue that experience of the soile, as thas there cannobee shewed anie reason to the contrary, but that it will grow there excellent well; and by planting will be yeelded plentifully : seeing there is so much ground whereof some may well be applyed to such purposes. What benefite heereof may growe in cordage and linnens who can not easily vnderstand?

## Allum.

There is a veine of earth along the sea coast for the space of fourtie or fiftie miles, whereof by the iudgement of some that haue made triall heere in England, is made good Allum, of that kinde which is called Roche Allum. The richnesse of such a commoditie is so well knowne that I neede not to saye any thing thereof. The same earth doth also yeelde White Copresse, Nitrum, and Alumen Plumeum, but nothing so plentifully as the common Allum; which be also of price and profitable.

## Wapeih.

Wapeih, a kinde of earth so called by the naturall inhabitants; very like to terra sigillata: and hauing beene refined, it hath beene found by some of our Phisitiós and Chirurgeons to bee of the same kinde of vertue and more effectuall. The inhabitãts vse it very much for the cure of sores and woundes : there is in diuers places great plentie, and in some places of a blewe sort.

## Pitch, Tarre, Rozen, and Turpentine.

There are those kindes of trees which yeelde them abundantly and great store. In the very same Iland where wee were seated, being fifteene miles of length, and fiue or sixe miles in breadth, there are fewe trees els but of the same kind; the whole Iland being full.

Sassafras.

## Saſſafras.

Saſſafras, called by the inhabitantes Winauk, a kinde of wood of moſt pleaſand and ſweete ſmel; and of moſt rare vertues in phiſick for the cure of many diſeaſes. It is found by experience to bee farre better and of more vſes then the wood which is called Guaiacum, or Lignum vitæ. For the deſcription, the manner of vſing and the manifolde vertues thereof, I referre you to the booke of Monardus, tranſlated and entituled in English, The ioyfull newes from the Weſt Indies.

## Cedar.

Cedar, a very ſweet wood & fine timber; wherof if neſts of cheſts be there made, or timber theroff fitted for ſweet & fine bedſteads, tables, deskes, lutes, virginalles & many things elſe, (of which there hath beene proofe made already) to make vp fraite with other principal commodities will yeeld profite.

## Wine.

There are two kinds of grapes that the ſoile doth yeeld naturally : the one is ſmall and ſowre of the ordinarie bigneſſe as ours in England: the other farre greater & of himſelfe iuſhious ſweet. When they are plãted and huſbandeg as they ought, a principall commoditie of wines by them may be raiſed.

## Oyle.

There are two ſortes of Walnuttes both holding oyle, but the one farre more plentifull then the other. When there are milles & other deuiſes for the purpoſe, a commodity of them may be raiſed becauſe there are infinite ſtore. There are alſo three ſeuerall kindes of Berries in the forme of Oke akornes, which alſo by the experience and vſe of the inhabitantes, wee finde to yeelde very good and ſweete oyle. Furthermore the Beares of the countrey are commonly very fatte, and in ſome places there are many: their fatneſſe becauſe it is ſo liquid, may well be termed oyle, and hath many ſpeciall vſes.

## Furres:

All along the Sea coaſt there are great ſtore of Otters, which beeyng taken by weares and other engines made for the purpoſe, will yeelde good profite. Wee hope alſo of Marterne furres, and make no doubt by the relation of the people but that in ſome places of the countrey there are ſtore: although there were but two skinnes that came to our handes. Luzarnes alſo we haue vnderſtãding of. although for the time we ſaw none.

## Deare skinnes.

Deare skinnes dreſſed after the manner of Chamoes or vndreſſed are to be had of the naturall inhabitants thouſands yeerely by way of trafficke for trifles : and no more waſt or ſpoile of Deare then is and hath beene ordinarily in time before.

## Ciuet cattes.

In our trauailes, there was founde one to haue beene killed by a ſaluage or inhabitant: and in an other place the ſmell where one or more had lately beene before: whereby we gather beſides then by the relation of the people that there are ſome in the countrey: good profite will riſe by them.

## Jron.

In two places of the countrey ſpecially, one about foureſcore and the other ſixe ſcore miles from the Fort or place where wee dwelt : wee founde neere the water ſide the ground to be rockie, which by the triall of a minerall man, was founde to holde Iron richly. It is founde in manie places of the countrey elſe. I knowe nothing to the contrarie, but that it maie bee allowed for a good marchantable commoditie, conſidering there the ſmall charge for the labour and feeding of men : the infinite ſtore of wood: the want of wood and decreneſſe thereof in England: & the neceſſity of ballaſting of ſhippes.

## Copper.

A hundred and fiftie miles into the maine in two townes wee founde with the inhabitaunts diuerſe ſmall plates of copper , that had beene made as wee vnderſtood, by the inhabitantes that dwell farther into the countrey : where as they ſay are mountaines and Riuers that yeelde alſo whyte graynes of Mettall, which is to bee deemed Siluer. For confirmation whereof at the time of our firſt arriuall in the Countrey, I ſawe with ſome others with mee, two ſmall peeces of ſiluer groſly beaten about the weight of a Teſtrone, hangyng in the eares of a Wiroans or chiefe Lorde that dwelt about foureſcore myles from vs ; of whom thorowe enquiry, by the number of dayes and the way , I learned that it had come to his handes from the ſame place or neere, where I after vnderſtood the copper was made and the white graynes of mettall founde. The aforeſaide copper wee alſo founde by triall to holde ſiluer.

## Pearle.

Sometimes in feeding on muſcles wee founde ſome pearle; but it was our hap to meete with ragges, or of a pide colour; not hauing yet diſcouered thoſe

places

places where wee hearde of better and more plentie. One of our companie; a man of skill in such matters, had gathered to gether from among the sauage people a-boute fiue thousande: of which number he chose so many as made a fayre chaine, which for their likenesse and vniformitie in roundnesse, orientnesse, and pidenesse of mãny excellent colours, with equalitie in greatnesse; were verie fayre and rare; and had therefore beene presented to her Maiestie , had wee not by casualtie and trough extremity of a storme, lost them with many things els in comming away from the countrey.

## Sweete Gummes.

Sweete Gummes of diuers kindes and many other Apothecary drugges of which wee will make speciall mention, when wee shall receiue it from such men of skill in that kynd, that in taking reasonable paines shall discouer them more parti-cularly then wee haue done; and than now I can make relation of, for want of the examples I had prouided and gathered , and are nowe lost, with other thinges by causualtie before mentioned.

## Dyes of diuers kindes.

There is Shoemake well knowen, and vsed in England for blacke; the seede of an hearbe called Wasewówr: little small rootes called Cháppacor; and the barke of the tree called by the inhabitaunts Tangomóckonomindge: which Dies are for diuers sortes of red: their goodnesse for our English clothes remayne yet to be pro-ued. The inhabitants vse them onely for the dying of hayre; and colouring of their faces, aud Mantles made of Deare skinnes; and also for the dying of Rushes to ma-ke artificiall workes withall in their Mattes and Baskettes; hauing no other thing besides that they account of, apt to vse them for. If they will not proue merchan-table there is no doubt but the Planters there shall finde apte vses for them, as also for other colours which wee knowe to be there.

## Oade.

A thing of so great vent and vse amongst English Diers, which cannot bee yeelded sufficiently in our owne countrey for spare of ground; may bee planted in Virginia, there being ground enough. The grouth therof need not to be doubted when as in the Ilandes of the Asores it groweth plentifully, which is in the same cli-mate. So likewise of Madder.

## Suger canes.

Whe carried thither Suger canes to plant which beeing not so well preserued as was requisit, & besides the time of the yere being past for their setting when we

arriued, wee could not make that proofe of them as wee defired. Notwithſtā ding
feeing that they grow in the ſame climate , in the South part of Spaine and in Bar-
bary, our hope in reaſon may yet continue.  So likewiſe for *Orenges* , and *Lemmons,*
there may be planted alſo *Quinſes*.  Wherbi may grow in reaſonable time if the a-
ction be diligently proſecuted, no ſmall commodities in *Sugers, Suckets,* and *Mar-*
*malades.*

 Many other commodities by planting may there alſo bee raiſed , which I leaue to your diſcret and gentle conſiderations : and many alſo may bee there which
yet we haue not diſcouered. Two more commodities of great value one of certaintie, and the other in hope , not to be planted ,  but there to be raiſed & in ſhort time
to be prouided and prepared, I might haue ſpecified. So likewiſe of thoſe commodities already ſet downe I might haue ſaid more ; as of the particular places where
they are founde and beſt to be planted and prepared : by what meanes and in what
reaſonable ſpace of time they might be raiſed to profit and in what proportion ; but
becauſe others then welwillers might bee therewithall acquainted, not to the good
  of the action, I haue wittingly omitted them : knowing that to thoſe that
   are well diſpoſed I haue vttered , according to my promiſe
    and purpoſe, for this part ſuffi-
     cient.

THE

THE SECOND PART,
## OF SVCHE COMMO-DITIES AS VIRGINIA IS
knowne to yeelde for victuall and suftenáce of mans
life, vfually fed vpon by the naturall inhabitants:
as alfo by vs during the time of our aboad.
And firft of fuch as are fowed
and husbanded.

AGATOWR, a kinde of graine fo called by the inhabitants ; the fame in the Weft Indies is called MAYZE: English men call it Guinney wheate or Turkie wheate, according to the names of the countreys from whence the like hath beene brought. The graine is about the bignefle of our ordinary English peaze and not much different in forme and fhape : but of diuers colours: fome white, fome red, fome yellow, and fome blew. All of them yeelde a very white and fweete flowre : beeing vfed according to his kinde it maketh a very good bread. Wee made of the fame in the countrey fome mault, whereof was brued as good ale as was to bee defired. So likewife by the help of hops therof may bee made as good Beere. It is a graine of marueilous great increafe; of a thoufand, fifteene hundred and fome two thoufand fold. There are three fortes, of which two are ripe in an eleuen and twelue weekes at the moft : fometimes in ten, after the time they are fet, and are then of height in ftalke about fixe or feuen foote. The other fort is ripe in fourtee-ne, and is about ten foote high, of the ftalkes fome beare foure heads, fome three, fome one, and two : euery head cótaining fiue, fixe, or feué hundred graines within a fewe more or leffe. Of thefe graines befides bread, the inhabitants make victuall

eyther by parching them; or seething them whole vntill they be broken; or boyling the floure with water into a pappe.

*Okindgier*, called by vs *Beanes*, because in greatnesse & partly in shape they are like to the Beanes in England; sauing that they are flatter, of more diuers colours, and some pide. The leafe also of the stemme is much different. In taste they are altogether as good as our English peaze.

*Wickonzówr*, called by vs *Peaze*, in respect of the beanes for distinction sake, because they are much lesse; although in forme they little differ; but in goodnesse of tast much, & are far better then our English peaze. Both the beanes and peaze are ripe in tenne weekes after they are set. They make them victuall either by boyling them all to pieces into a broth; or boiling them whole vntill they bee soft and beginne to breake as is vsed in England, eyther by themselues or mixtly together: Sometime they mingle of the wheate with them. Sometime also beeing whole soddeu, they bruse or pound them in a morter, & thereof make loaues or lumps of dowishe bread, which they vse to eat for varietie.

*Macócqwer*, according to their feuerall formes called by vs, *Pompions*, *Mellions*, and *Gourdes*, because they are of the like formes as those kindes in England. In *Virginia* such of feuerall formes are of one taste and very good, and do also spring from one feed. There are of two forts; one is ripe in the space of a moneth, and the other in two moneths.

There is an hearbe which in Dutch is called *Melden*. Some of those that I describe it vnto, take it to be a kinde of Orage; it groweth about foure or fiue foote high: of the feede thereof they make a thicke broth, and pottage of a very good taste: of the stalke by burning into ashes they make a kinde of salt earth, wherewithall many vse sometimes to season their brothes; other salte they knowe not. Wee our selues, vsed the leaues also for pothearbes.

There is also another great hearbe in forme of a Marigolde, about sixe foote in height; the head with the floure is a spanne in breadth. Some take it to bee *Planta Solis*: of the feedes heereof they make both a kinde of bread and broth.

All the aforesaide commodities for victuall are fet or sowed, sometimes in groundes a part and feuerally by themselues; but for the most part together in one ground mixtly : the manner thereof with the dressing and preparing of the groud, because I will note vnto you the fertilitie of the foile; I thinke good briefly to describe.

The ground they neuer fatten with mucke, dounge or any other thing; neither plow nor digge it as we in England, but onely prepare it in fort as followeth. A fewe daies before they fowe or fet, the men with wooden instruments, made almost in forme of mattockes or hoes with long handles; the women with short peckers or parers, because they vse them fitting, of a foote long and about fiue inches in breadth : doe onely breake the vpper part of the ground to rayse vp the weedes, grasse, & old stubbes of corne stalkes with their rootes. The which after a day or twoes

drying

drying in the Sunne, being ſcrapte vp into many ſmall heapes, to ſaue them labour for carrying them away; they burne into aſhes. (And whereas ſome may thinke that they vſe the aſhes for to better the grounde; I ſay that then they woulde eyther diſperſe the aſhes abroade; which wee obſerued they doe not, except the heapes bee too great: or els would take ſpeciall care to ſet their corne where the aſhes lie, which alſo wee finde they are careleſſe of.) And this is all the huſbanding of their ground that they vſe.

Then their ſetting or ſowing is after this maner. Firſt for their corne, beginning in one corner of the plot, with a pecker they make a hole, wherein they put foure graines with that care they touch not one another, (about an inch aſunder) and couer them with the moulde againe: and ſo through out the whole plot, making ſuch holes and vſing them after ſuch maner: but with this regard that they bee made in rankes, euery rāke differing from other halfe a fadome or a yarde, and the holes alſo in euery ranke, as much. By this meanes there is a yarde ſpare ground betwene euery hole: where according to diſcretion here and there, they ſet as many Beanes and Peaze: in diuers places alſo among the ſeedes of *Macócqwer, Melden* and *Planta Solis.*

The ground being thus ſet according to the rate by vs experimented, an Engliſh Acre conteining fourtie pearches in length, and foure in breadth, doeth there yeeld in croppe or oſcome of corne, beanes, and peaze, at the leaſt two hūdred London buſhelles: beſides the *Macócqwer, Melden,* and *Planta Solis*: When as in England fourtie buſhelles of our wheate yeelded out of ſuch an acre is thought to be much.

I thought alſo good to note this vnto you, if you which ſhall inhabite and plant there, maie know how ſpecially that countrey corne is there to be preferred before ours: Beſides the manifold waies in applying it to victuall, the increaſe is ſo much that ſmall labour and paines is needful in reſpect that muſt be vſed for ours. For this I can aſſure you that according to the rate we haue made proofe of, one man may prepare and huſbane ſo much grounde (hauing once borne corne before) with leſſe thē foure and twentie houres labour, as ſhall yeelde him victuall in a large proportiō for a twelue mōeth, if hee haue nothing elſe, but that which the ſame groūd will yeelde, and of that kinde onelie which I haue before ſpoken of: the ſaide groūd being alſo but of fiue and twentie yards ſquare. And if neede require, but that there is ground enough, there might be raiſed out of one and the ſelfſame ground two harueſtes or oſcomes; for they ſowe or ſet and may at anie time when they thinke good from the middeſt of March vntill the ende of Iune: ſo that they alſo ſet when they haue eaten of their firſt croppe. In ſome places of the countrey notwithſtanding they haue two harueſts, as we haue heard, out of one and the ſame ground.

For Engliſh corne neuertheles whether to vſe or not to vſe it, you that inhabite maie do as you ſhall haue farther cauſe to thinke beſt. Of the grouth you need not to doubt: for barlie, oates and peaze, we haue ſeene proof of, not beeing purpoſely sowen but fallen casually in the worst sort of ground, and yet to be as faire as any we haue euer seene here in England. But of wheat because it was musty and hat taken salt water wee could make no triall : and of rye we had none. Thus much haue I digressed and I hope not vnnecessarily: nowe will I returne againe to my course and intreate of that which yet remaineth appertaining to this Chapter.

There is an herbe which is sowed a part by it selfe & is called by the inhabitants Vppówoc: In the West Indies it hath diuers names, according to the seuerall places & countries where it groweth and is vsed : The Spaniardes generally call it Tobacco. The leaues thereof being dried and brought into powder: they vse to take the fume or smoke thereof by sucking it through pipes made of claie into their stomacke and heade; from whence it purgeth superfluous fleame & other grosse humors, openeth all the pores & passages of the body: by which meanes the vse thereof, not only preserueth the body from obstructiós; but also if any be, so that they haue not beene of too long continuance, in short time breaketh them: wherby their bodies are notably preserued in health, & know not many greeuous diseases wherewithall wee in England are oftentimes afflicted.

This Vppówoc is of so precious estimation amongest then, that they thinke their gods are marueloufly delighted therwith: Wherupon sometime they make hallowed fires & cast some of the pouder therein for a sacrifice : being in a storme vppon the waters, to pacifie their gods, they cast some vp into the aire and into the water: so a weare for fish being newly set vp, they cast some therein and into the aire: also after an escape of danger, they cast some into the aire likewise : but all done with strange gestures, stamping, somtime dauncing, clapping of hands, holding vp of hands, & staring vp into rhe heauens, vttering therewithal and chattering str ge words & noises.

We our selues during the time we were there vsed to suck it after their maner, as also since our returne , & haue found maine rare and wonderful experiments of the vertues thereof; of which the relation woulde require a volume by it selfe : the vse of it by so manie of late, men & women of great calling as else, and some learned Phisitions also, is sufficient witnes.

And these are all the commodities for sustenance of life that I know and can remember they vse to husband: all else that followe are founde growing naturally or wilde.

## Of Rootes.

O P E N A V K are a kind of roots of round forme , some of the bignes of walnuts, some far greater, which are found in moist & marish grounds growing many together one by another in ropes, or as thogh they were fastnened with a string. Being boiled or sodden they are very good meate.

O K E E P E N A V K are also of round shape, found in dry grounds : some are of the of the bignes of a mans head.　They are to be eaten as they are taken out of the ground, for by reason of their drinesse they will neither roste nor seeth.　Their tast is not so good as of the former rootes, notwithstanding for want of bread & somtimes for varietie the inhabitants vse to eate them with fish or flesh, and in my iudgement they doe as well as the houshold bread made of rie heere in England.

*Kaishúcpenauk* a white kind of roots about the bignes of hen egs & nere of that forme: their tast was not so good to our seeming as of the other, and therfore their place and manner of growing not so much cared for by vs: the inhabitāts notwithstanding vsed to boile & eate many.

*Tsinaw* a kind of roote much like vnto the which in England is called the *China root* brought from the East Indies.　And we know not anie thing to the cōtrary but that it maie be of the same kind. These roots grow manie together in great clusters. and doe bring foorth a brier stalke, but the leafe in shape far vnlike; which beeing supported by the trees it groweth neerest vnto, wil reach or climbe to the top of the highest. From these roots while they be new or fresh beeing chopt into small pieces & stampt, is strained with water a iuice that maketh bread, & also being boiled, a very good spoonemeate in maner of a gelly, and is much better in tast if it bee tempered with oyle. This *Tsinaw* is not of that sort which by some was caused to be brought into England for the *China roote*, for it was discouered since, and is in vse as is aforesaide: but that which was brought hither is not yet knowne neither by vs nor by the inhabitants to serue for any vse or purpose; although the rootes in shape are very like.

*Coscúshaw*, some of our company tooke to bee that kinde of roote which the Spaniards in the West Indies call *Cassauy*, whereupon also many called it by that name: it groweth in very muddie pooles and moist groundes. Being dressed according to the countrey maner, it maketh a good bread, and also a good sponemeate, and is vsed very much by the inhabitants: The iuice of this root is poison, and therefore heede must be taken before any thing be made therewithal : Either the rootes must bee first sliced and dried in the Sunne, or by the fire, and then being pounded into floure wil make good bread : or els while they are greene they are to bee pared, cut into pieces and stampt; loues of the same to be laid neere or ouer the fire vntill it be soure, and then being well pounded againe, bread, or spone meate very good in taste, and holsome may be made thereof.

*Habascon* is a roote of hoat taste almost of the forme and bignesse of a Parseneepe, of it selfe it is no victuall, but onely a helpe beeing boiled together with other meates.

　　There are also *Leekes* differing little from ours in England that grow in ma
　　ny places of the countrey, of which, when we came in places where,
　　　wee gathered and eate many, but the naturall
　　　　　inhabitants neuer.

## Of Fruites.

CHESTNVTS, there are in diuers places great ſtore: ſome they vſe to eate ra-
we, ſome they ſtampe and boile to make ſpoonemeate, and with ſome being ſod-
den they make ſuch a manner of dowe bread as they vſe of their beanes before
mentioned.

WALNVTS: There are two kindes of Walnuts, and of then infinit ſtore: In
many places where very great woods for many miles together the third part of trees are walnuttrees. The one kind is of the ſame taſte and forme or litle differing
from ours of England, but that they are harder and thicker ſhelled: the other is
greater and hath a verie ragged and harde ſhell: but the kernell great, verie oylie
and ſweete. Beſides their eating of them after our ordinarie maner, they breake
them with ſtones and pound them in morters with water to make a milk which
they vſe to put into ſome ſorts of their ſpoonmeate; alſo among their ſodde wheat,
peaze, beanes and pompions which maketh them haue a farre more pleaſant taſte.

MEDLARS a kind of verie good fruit, ſo called by vs chieflie for theſe re-
ſpectes: firſt in that they are not good vntill they be rotten: then in that they open
at the head as our medlars, and are about the ſame bigneſſe: otherwiſe in taſte and
colour they are farre differēt: for they are as red as cheries and very ſweet: but whereas the cherie is ſharpe ſweet, they are luſhious ſweet.

METAQVESVNNAVK, a kinde of pleaſaunt fruite almoſt of the ſhape &
bignes of Engliſh peares, but that they are of a perfect red colour as well within as
without. They grow on a plant whoſe leaues are verie thicke and full of prickles as
ſharpe as needles. Some that haue bin in the Indies, where they haue ſeen that kind
of red die of great price which is called Cochinile to grow, doe deſcribe his plant
right like vnto this of Metaqueſûnnauk but whether it be the true Cochinile or a
baſtard or wilde kind, it cannot yet be certified; ſeeing that alſo as I heard, Cochinile is not of the fruite but founde on the leaues of the plant; which leaues for ſuch
matter we haue not ſo ſpecially obſerued.

GRAPES there are of two ſorts which I mentioned in the marchantable cōmodities.

STRABERIES there are as good & as great as thoſe which we haue in our
Engliſh gardens.

MVLBERIES, Applecrabs, Hurts or Hurtleberies, ſuch as wee haue in
England.

SACQVENVMMENER a kinde of berries almoſt like vnto capres but ſo-
mewhat greater which grow together in cluſters vpon a plant or herb that is found
in ſhalow waters: being boiled eight or nine hours according to their kind are very good meate and holeſome, otherwiſe if they be eaten they will make a man for
the time franticke or extremely ſicke.

There is a kind of reed which beareth a ſeed almoſt like vnto our rie or wheat,
& being boiled is good meate.

In

In our trauailes in some places wee founde *wilde peaze* like vnto ours in England but that they were lesse, which are also good meate.

## *Of a kinde of fruite or berrie in forme of Acornes.*

There is a kind of berrie or acorne, of which there are fiue sorts that grow on seuerall kinds of trees; the one is called *Sagatémener*, the second *Osamener*, the third *Pummuckóner*. These kind of acorns they vse to drie vpon hurdles made of reeds with fire vnderneath almost after the maner as we dry malt in England. When they are to be vsed they first water them vntil they be soft & then being sod they make a good victuall, either to eate so simply, or els being also pounded, to make loaues or lumpes of bread. These be also the three kinds of which, I said before, the inhabitants vsed to make sweet oyle.

An other sort is called *Sapúmmener* which being boiled or parched doth eate and taste like vnto chestnuts. They sometime also make bread of this sort.

The fifth sort is called *Mangúmmenauk*, and is the acorne of their kind of oake, the which beeing dried after the maner of the first sortes, and afterward watered they boile them, & their seruants or sometime the chiefe theselues, either for varietie or for want of bread, doe eate them with their fish or flesh.

## *Of Beastes.*

*Deare*, in some places there are great store: neere vnto the sea coast they are of the ordinarie bignes as ours in England, & some lesse: but further vp into the countrey where there is better feed they are greater: they differ from ours onely in this, their tailes are longer and the snags of their hornes looke backward.

*Conies*, Those that we haue seen & al that we can heare of are of a grey colour like vnto hares: in some places there are such plétie that all the people of some townes make them mantles of the furre or flue of the skinnes of those they vsually take.

*Saquenúckot* & *Maquówoc*; two kindes of small beastes greater then conies which are very good meat. We neuer tooke any of them our selues, but sometime eate of such as the inhabitants had taken & brought vnto vs.

*Squirels* which are of a grey colour, we haue taken & eaten.

*Beares* which are all of black colour. The beares of this countrey are good meat; the inhabitants in time of winter do vse to take & eate manie, so also somtime did wee. They are taken cómonlie in this sort. In some Ilands or places where they are, being hunted for, as soone as they haue spiall of a man they presently run awaie, & then being chased they clime and get vp the next tree they can, from whence with arrowes they are shot downe starke dead, or with those wounds that they may after easily be killed; we sometime shotte them downe with our caleeuers.

I haue the names of eight & twenty feuerall fortes of beafts which I haue heard of to be here and there difperfed in the countrie, efpecially in the maine: of which there are only twelue kinds that we haue yet difcouered, & of thofe that be good meat we know only them before mentioned. The inhabitánts fomtime kil the *Lyon* & eat him: & we fomtime as they came to our hands of their *Wolues* or *woluish Dogges*, which I haue not fet downe for good meat, leaft that fome woulde vnderftand my iudgement therin to be more fimple than needeth, although I could alleage the difference in tafte of thofe kindes from ours, which by fome of our company haue beene experimented in both.

## Of Foule.

*Turkie cockes* and *Turkie hennes*: *Stockdoues*: *Partridges*: *Cranes*: *Hernes*: & in winter great ftore of *Swannes* & *Geefe*. Of al fortes of foule I haue the names in the countrie language of four efcore and fixe of which number befides thofe that be named, we haue taken, eaten, & haue the pictures as they were there drawne with the names of the inhabitaunts of feuerall ftrange fortes of water foule eight, and feuenteene kinds more of land foul, although wee haue feen and eaten of many more, which for want of leafure there for the purpofe coulde not bee pictured: and after wee are better furnished and ftored vpon further difcouety, with their ftrange beaftes, fishe, trees, plants, and hearbes, they shall bee alfo published.

There are alfo *Parats*, *Faulcons*, & *Marlin haukes*, which although with vs they bee not vfed for meate, yet for other caufes I thought good to mention.

## Of Fishe.

For foure monethes of the yeere, February, March, Aprill and May, there are plentie of *Sturgeons*: And alfo in the fame monethes of *Herrings*, fome of the ordinary bigneffe as ours in England, but the moft part farre greater, of eighteene, twentie inches, and fome two foote in length and better; both thefe kindes of fishe in thofe monethes are moft plentifull, and in beft feafon, which wee founde to bee moft delicate and pleafaunt meate.

There are alfo *Troutes*, *Porpoifes*, *Rayes*, *Oldwiues*, *Mullets*, *Plaice*, and very many other fortes of excellent good fish, which we haue taken & eaten, whofe names I know not but in the countrey language; wee haue of twelue forts more the pictures as they were drawn in the countrey with their names.

The inhabitants vfe to take then two maner of wayes, the one is by a kind of wear made of reedes which in that countrey are very ftrong. The other way which is more ftrange, is with poles made sharpe at one ende, by shooting them into the fish after the maner as Irishmen caft dartes; either as they are rowing in their boates or els as they are wading in the shallowes for the purpofe.

There

There are also in many places plentie of these kindes which follow.

*Sea crabbes*, such as we haue in England.

*Oystres*, some very great, and some small; some rounde and some of a long shape : They are founde both in salt water and brackish, and those that we had out of salt water are far better than the other as in our owne countrey.

Also *Muscles, Scalopes, Periwinkles*, and *Creuises*.

*Seekanauk*, a kinde of crustie shell fishe which is good meate, about a foote in breadth, hauing a crustie tayle, many legges like a crab; and her eyes in her backe. They are founde in shallowes of salt waters; and sometime on the shoare.

There are many *Tortoyses* both of lande and sea kinde, their backes & bellies are shelled very thicke; their head, feete, and taile, which are in appearance, seeme ougly as though they were membres of a serpent or venemous: but notwithstanding they are very good meate, as also their egges. Some haue bene founde of a yard in bredth and better.

And thus haue I made relation of all sortes of victuall that we fed vpon for the time we were in *Virginia*, as also the inhabitants themselues, as farre foorth as I knowe and can remember or that are specially worthy to bee remembred.

c

## THE THIRD AND
### LAST PART,

# OF SVCH OTHER
## THINGES AS IS BE HOO-

full for those which shall plant and inhabit to
know of; with a description of the nature
and manners of the people of
the countrey.

*Of commodities for building and other*
*necessary vses:*

Hose other things which I am more to make rehear-
fall of, are such as concerne building, and other mecha-
nicall necessarie vses; as diuers sortes of trees for house
& ship timber, and other vses els: Also lime, stone, and
brick, least that being not mentioned some might haue bene doubted of, or by some that are malicious re-
ported the contrary.

    *Okes*, there are as faire, straight, tall, and as good
timber as any can be, and also great store, and in some
places very great.

    W*alnut trees*, as I haue saide before very many, some haue bene seen excellent
faire timber of foure & fiue fadome, & aboue fourescore foot streight without
bough.

    *Firre trees* fit for masts of ships, some very tall & great.

*Rakiock,*

*Rakiock,* a kind of trees so called that are sweet wood of which the inhabitans that were neere vnto vs doe commonly make their boats or Canoes of the form of trowes; only with the helpe of fire, harchets of stones, and shels; we haue known some so great being made in that sort of one tree that they haue carried well x x. men at once, besides much baggage : the timber being great, tal, streight, soft, light, & yet tough enough I thinke (besides other vses) to be fit also for masts of ships.

*Cedar,* a sweet wood good for seelings, Chests, Boxes, Bedsteedes, Lutes, Virginals, and many things els, as I haue also said before. Some of our company which haue wandered in some places where I haue not bene, haue made certaine affirmation of *Cyprus* which for such and other excellent vses, is also a wood of price and no small estimation.

*Maple,* and also *Wich-hazle,* wherof the inhabitants vse to make their bowes.

*Holly* a necessary thing for the making of birdlime.

*Willowes* good for the making of weares and weeles to take fish after the English manner, although the inhabitants vse only reedes, which because they are so strong as also flexible, do serue for that turne very well and sufficiently.

*Beech* and *Ashe,* good for caske, hoopes : and if neede require, plow worke, as also for many things els.

*Elme.*

*Sassafras* trees.

*Ascopo* a kinde of tree very like vnto Lawrell, the barke is hoat in tast and spicie, it is very like to that tree which Monardus describeth to bee *Cassia Lignea* of the West Indies.

There are many other strange trees whose names I knowe not but in the *Virginian* language, of which I am not nowe able, neither is it so conuenient for the present to trouble you with particular relatiõ: seeing that for timber and other necessary vses I haue named sufficient : And of many of the rest but that they may be applied to good vse, I know no cause to doubt.

Now for Stone, Bricke and Lime, thus it is. Neere vnto the Sea coast where wee dwelt, there are no kinde of stones to bee found (except a fewe small pebbles about foure miles off) but such as haue bene brought from farther out of the maine. In some of our voiages wee haue seene diuers hard raggie stones, great pebbles, and a kinde of grey stone like vnto marble, of which the inhabitants make their hatchets to cleeue wood. Vpon inquirie wee heard that a little further vp into the Countrey were of all sortes verie many, although of Quarries they are ignorant, neither haue they vse of any store whereupon they should haue occasion to seeke any. For if euerie housholde haue one or two to cracke Nuttes, grinde shelles, whet copper, and sometimes other stones for hatchets, they haue enough : neither vse they any digging, but onely for graues about three foote deepe : and therefore no maruaile that they know neither Quarries, nor lime stones, which both may bee in places neerer than they wot of.

In the meane time vntill there bee difcouerie of fufficient ftore in fome place or other conuenient, the want of you which are and fhalbe the planters therein may be as well fupplied by Bricke : for the making whereof in diuers places of the countrey there is clay both excellent good, and plentie ; and alfo by lime made of Oifter fhels, and of others burnt, after the maner as they vfe in the Iles of Tenet and Shepy, and alfo in diuers other places of England: Which kinde of lime is well knowne to bee as good as any other. And of Oifter fhels there is plentie enough: for befides diuers other particular places where are abundance, there is one fhallowe founde along the coaft, where for the fpace of many miles together in lenght, and two or three miles in breadth, the grounde is nothing els beeing but halfe a foote or a foote vnder water for the moft part.

This much can I fay further more of ftones, that about 120. miles from our fort neere the water in the fide of a hill was founde by a Gentleman of our company, a great veine of hard ragge ftones, which I thought good to remember vnto you.

## Of the nature and manners of the people

It refteth I fpeake a word or two of the naturall inhabitants, their natures and maners, leauing large difcourfe thereof vntill time more conuenient hereafter : nowe onely fo farre foorth, as that you may know, how that they in refpect of troubling our inhabiting and planting, are not to be feared; but that they fhall haue caufe both to feare and loue vs, that fhall inhabite with them.

They are a people clothed with loofe mantles made of Deere skins, & aprons of the fame rounde about their middles; all els naked; of fuch a difference of ftatures only as wee in England ; hauing no edge tooles or weapons of yron or fteele to offend vs withall, neither know they how to make any: thofe weapos that they haue, are onlie bowes made of Witch hazle, & arrowes of reeds ; flat edged truncheons alfo of wood about a yard long, neither haue they any thing to defend themfelues but targets made of barcks ; and fome armours made of ftickes wickered together with thread.

Their townes are but fmall, & neere the fea coaft but few, fome cotaining but 10. or 12. houfes: fome 20. the greateft that we haue feene haue bene but of 30. houfes: if they be walled it is only done with barks of trees made faft to ftakes, or els with poles onely fixed vpright and clofe one by another.

Their houfes are made of fmall poles made faft at the tops in rounde forme after the maner as is vfed in many arbories in our gardens of England, in moft townes couered with barkes, and in fome with artificiall mattes made of long rushes; from the tops of the houfes downe to the ground. The length of them is commonly double to the breadth, in fome places they are but 12. and 16. yardes long, and in other fome wee haue feene of foure and twentie.

In

In some places of the countrey one onely towne belongeth to the gouern-ment of a *Wiróans* or chiefe Lorde; in other some two or three, in some sixe, eight, & more; the greatest *Wiróans* that yet we had dealing with had but eighteene tow-nes in his gouernmēt, and able to make not aboue seuen or eight hundred fighting men at the most: The language of euery gouernment is different from any other, and the farther they are distant the greater is the difference.

Their maner of warres amongst themselues is either by sudden surprising one an other most commonly about the dawning of the day, or moone light; or els by ambushes, or some suttle deuises : Set battels are very rare, except it fall out where there are many trees, where eyther part may haue some hope of defence, after the deliuerie of euery arrow, in leaping behind some or other.

If there fall out any warres betwee vs & them, what their fight is likely to bee, we hauing aduantages against them so many maner of waies, as by our discipline, our strange weapons and deuises els; especially by ordinance great and small, it may be easily imagined ; by the experience we haue had in some places, the turning vp of their heeles against vs in running away was their best defence.

In respect of vs they are a people poore, and for want of skill and iudgement in the knowledge and vse of our things, doe esteeme our trifles before thinges of greater value: Notwithstanding in their proper manner considering the want of such meanes as we haue, they seeme very ingenious ; For although they haue no such tooles, nor any such craftes, sciences and artes as wee ; yet in those thinges they doe, they shewe excellencie of wit. And by howe much they vpon due considera-tion shall finde our manner of knowledges and craftes to exceede theirs in perfe-ction, and speed for doing or execution, by so much the more is it probable that they shoulde desire our friendships & loue, and haue the greater respect for plea-sing and obeying vs. Whereby may bee hoped if meanes of good gouernment bee vsed, that they may in short time be brought to ciuilitie, and the imbracing of true religion.

Some religion they haue alreadie, which although it be farre from the truth, yet beyng at it is, there is hope it may bee the easier and sooner reformed.

They beleeue that there are many Gods which they call *Mantóac*, but of dif-ferent sortes and degrees; one onely chiefe and great God, which hath bene from all eternitie. Who as they affirme when hee purposed to make the worlde, made first other goddes of a principall order to bee as meanes and instruments to bee v-sed in the creation and gouernment to follow; and after the Sunne, Moone, and Starres, as pettie goddes and the instruments of the other order more principall. First they say were made waters, out of which by the gods was made all diuersitie of creatures that are visible or inuisible.

For mankind they say a woman was made first, which by the woorking of one of the goddes, conceiued and brought foorth children : And in such sort they say they had their beginning.

But how manie yeeres or ages haue paſſed ſince, they ſay they can make no re-lation, hauing no letters nor other ſuch meanes as we to keepe recordes of the par-ticularities of times paſt, but onelie tradition from father to ſonne.

They thinke that all the gods are of humane ſhape, & therfore they repreſent them by images in the formes of men, which they call *Kewaſowok* one alone is cal-led *Kewás*; Them they place in houſes appropriate or temples which they call *Mathicómuck*; Where they woorſhip, praie, ſing, and make manie times offerings vnto them. In ſome *Machicómuck* we haue ſeene but on *Kewas*, in ſome two, and in other ſome three; The common ſort thinke them to be alſo gods.

They beleeue alſo the immortalitie of the ſoule, that after this life as ſoone as the ſoule is departed from the bodie according to the workes it hath done, it is ey-ther carried to heauē the habitacle of gods, there to enioy perpetuall bliſſe and hap-pineſſe, or els to a great pitte or hole, which they thinke to bee in the furtheſt partes of their part of the worlde towarde the ſunne ſet, there to burne continually: the place they call *Popoguſſo*.

For the confirmation of this opinion, they tolde mee two ſtories of two men that had been lately dead and reuiued againe, the one happened but few yeres be-fore our comming in the countrey of a wicked man which hauing beene dead and buried, the next day the earth of the graue beeing ſeene to moue, was takē vp agai-ne; Who made declaration where his ſoule had beene, that is to ſaie very neere en-tring into *Popoguſſo*, had not one of the gods ſaued him & gaue him leaue to retur-ne againe, and teach his friends what they ſhould doe to auoid that terrible place of torment.

The other happenē in the ſame yeere wee were there, but in a towne that was threeſcore miles from vs, and it was tolde mee for ſtraunge newes that one beeing dead, buried and taken vp againe as the firſt, ſhewed that although his bodie had lien dead in the graue, yet his ſoule was aliue, and had trauailed farre in a long broa-de waie, on both ſides whereof grewe moſt delicate and pleaſaūt trees, bearing mo-re rare and excellent fruites then euer hee had ſeene before or was able to expreſſe, and at length came to moſt braue and faire houſes, neere which hee met his father, that had beene dead before, who gaue him great charge to goe backe againe and ſhew his friendes what good they were to doe to enioy the pleaſures of that place, which when he had done he ſhould after come againe.

What ſubtilty ſoeuer be in the *Wiroances* and Prieſtes, this opinion worketh ſo much in manie of the common and ſimple ſort of people that it maketh them ha-ue great reſpect to their Gouernours, and alſo great care what they do, to auoid tor-ment after death, and to enioy bliſſe; althought notwithſtanding there is puniſh-ment ordained for malefactours, as ſtealers, whoremoongers, and other ſortes of wicked doers; ſome puniſhed with death, ſome with forfeitures, ſome with beating, according to the greatnes of the factes.

And this is the ſumme of their religion, which I learned by hauing ſpecial fa-
miliarity

miliarity with some of their priestes. Wherein they were not so sure grounded, nor gaue such credite to their traditions and stories but through conuersing with vs they were brought into great doubts of their owne, and no small admiratio of ours, with earnest desire in many, to learne more than we had meanes for want of perfect vtterance in their language to expresse.

Most thinges they sawe with vs, as Mathematicall instruments, sea compasses, the vertue of the loadstone in drawing yron, a perspectiue glasse whereby was shewed manie strange sightes, burning glasses, wildefire woorkes, gunnes, bookes, writing and reading, spring clocks that seeme to goe of themselues, and manie other thinges that wee had, were so straunge vnto them, and so farre exceeded their capacities to comprehend the reason and meanes how they should be made and done, that they thought they were rather the works of gods then of men, or at the leastwise they had bin giuen and taught vs of the gods. Which made manie of them to haue such opinion of vs, as that if they knew not the trueth of god and religion already, it was rather to be had from vs, whom God so specially loued then from a people that were so simple, as they found themselues to be in comparison of vs. Whereupon greater credite was giuen vnto that we spake of concerning such matters.

Manie times and in euery towne where I came, according as I was able, I made declaration of the contentes of the Bible; that therein was set foorth the true and onelie G o D, and his mightie woorkes, that therein was contayned the true doctrine of saluation through Christ, with manie particularities of Miracles and chiefe poyntes of religion, as I was able then to vtter, and thought fitte for the time. And although I told them the booke materially & of it self was not of anie such vertue, as I thought they did conceiue, but onely the doctrine therein cōtained; yet would many be glad to touch it, to embrace it, to kisse it, to hold it to their brests and heades, and stroke ouer all their bodie with it; to shewe their hungrie desire of that knowledge which was spoken of.

The Wiroans with whom we dwelt called Wingina, and many of his people would be glad many times to be with vs at our praiers, and many times call vpon vs both in his owne towne, as also in others whither he sometimes accompanied vs, to pray and sing Psalmes; hoping thereby to bee partaker of the same effectes which wee by that meanes also expected.

Twise this Wiroans was so grieuously sicke that he was like to die, and as hee laie languishing, doubting of anie helpe by his owne priestes, and thinking he was in such daunger for offending vs and thereby our god, sent for some of vs to praie and bee a meanes to our God that it would please him either that he might liue or after death dwell with him in blisse, so likewise were the requestes of manie others in the like case.

On a time also when their corne began to wither by reason of a drouth which happened extraordinarily, fearing that it had come to passe by reason that in some thing they had displeased vs, many woulde come to vs & desire vs to praie to our God of England, that he would preserue their corne, promising that when it was ripe we also should be partakers of the fruite.

There could at no time happen any strange sicknesse, losses, hurtes, or any other crosse vnto them, but that they would impute to vs the cause or meanes therof for offending or not pleasing vs.

One other rare and strange accident, leauing others, will I mention before I ende, which mooued the whole countrey that either knew or hearde of vs, to haue vs in wonderfull admiration.

There was no towne where we had any subtile deuise practised against vs, we leauing it vnpunished or not reuenged (because wee sought by all meanes possible to win them by gentlenesse) but that within a few dayes after our departure from euerie such towne, the people began to die very fast, and many in short space; in some townes about twentie, in some fourtie, in some sixtie, & in one sixe score, which in trueth was very manie in respect of their numbers. This happened in no place that wee coulde learne but where wee had bene, where they vsed some practise against vs, and after such time; The disease also so strange, that they neither knew what it was, nor how to cure it, the like by report of the oldest men in the countrey neuer happened before, time out of minde. A thing specially obserued by vs as also by the naturall inhabitants themselues.

Insomuch that when some of the inhabitants which were our friends & especially the *Wiroans Wingina* had obserued such effects in foure or fiue towns to follow their wicked practises, they were perswaded that it was the worke of our God through our meanes, and that wee by him might kil and slai whom wee would without weapons and not come neere them.

And thereupon when it had happened that they had vnderstanding that any of their enemies had abused vs in our iourneyes, hearing that wee had wrought no reuenge with our weapons, & fearing vpon some cause the matter should so rest: did come and intreate vs that we woulde bee a meanes to our God that they as others that had dealt ill with vs might in like sort die; alleaging howe much it would be for our credite and profite, as also theirs; and hoping furthermore that we would do so much at their requests in respect of the friendship we professe them.

Whose entreaties although wee shewed that they were vngodlie, affirming that our God would not subiect him selfe to anie such praiers and requestes of mē: that in deede all thinges haue beene and were to be done according to his good pleasure as he had ordained: ād that we to shew our selues his true seruāts ought rather to make petition for the contrarie, that they with them might liue together with vs, bee made partakers of his truth & serue him in righteousnes; but notwithstanding in such sort, that wee referre that as all other thinges, to bee done according to his diuine will & pleasure, ād as by his wisedome he had ordained to be best.

                                                       Yet

Yet becaufe the effect fell out fo fodainly and fhortly after according to their defires, they thought neuerthelefle it came to pafle by our meanes, and that we in vfing fuch fpeeches vnto them did but diffemble the matter, and therefore came vnto vs to giue vs thankes in their manner that although wee fatisfied them not in promife, yet in deedes and effect we had fulfilled their defires.

This maruelous accident in all the countrie wrought fo ftrange opinions of vs, that fome people could not tel whether to think vs gods or men, and the rather becaufe that all the fpace of their ficknefle, there was no man of ours knowne to die, or that was fpecially ficke: they noted alfo that we had no women amongft vs, neither that we did care for any of theirs.

Some therefore were of opinion that wee were not borne of women, and therefore not mortall, but that wee were men of an old generation many yeeres paft then rifen againe to immortalitie.

Some woulde likewife feeme to prophefie that there were more of our generation yet to come, to kill theirs and take their places, as fome thought the purpofe was by that which was already done.

Thofe that were immediatly to come after vs they imagined to be in the aire, yet inuifible & without bodies, & that they by our intreaty & for the loue of vs did make the people to die in that fort as they did by fhooting inuifible bullets into them.

To confirme this opinion their phifitions to excufe their ignorance in curing the difeafe, would not be afhemed to fay, but earneftly make the fimple people beleue, that the ftrings of blood that they fucked out of the ficke bodies, were the ftrings wherewithal the inuifible bullets were tied and caft.

Some alfo thought that we fhot them our felues out of our pieces from the place where we dwelt, and killed the people in any fuch towne that had offended vs as we lifted, how farre diftant from vs foeuer it were.

And other fome faide that it was the fpeciall woorke of God for our fakes, as wee our felues haue caufe in fome forte to thinke no lefle, whatfoeuer fome doe or maie imagine to the contrarie, fpecially fome Aftrologers knowing of the Eclipfe of the Sunne which wee faw the fame yeere before in our voyage thytherward, which vnto them appeared very terrible. And alfo of a Comet which beganne to appeare but a few daies before the beginning of the faid ficknefle. But to exclude them from being the fpeciall an accident, there are farther reafons then I thinke fit at this prefent to bee alleadged.

Thefe their opinions I haue fet downe the more at large that it may appeare vnto you that there is good hope they may be brought through difcreet dealing and gouernement to the imbracing of the trueth, and confequently to honour, obey, feare and loue vs.

d

And although some of our companie towardes the ende of the yeare, shewed themselues too fierce, in slaying some of the people, in some towns, vpō causes that on our part, might easily enough haue been borne withall: yet notwithstanding because it was on their part iustly deserued, the alteration of their opinions generally & for the most part concerning vs is the lesse to bee doubted. And whatsoeuer els they may be, by carefulnesse of our selues neede nothing at all to be feared.

The best neuerthelesse in this as in all actions besides is to be endeuoured and hoped, & of the worst that may happen notice to bee taken with consideration, and as much as may be eschewed.

The

## The Conclusion.

Now I haue as I hope made relation not of so fewe and smal things but that the countrey of men that are indifferent & wel disposed maie be sufficiently liked: If there were no more knowen then I haue mentioned, which doubtlesse and in great reason is nothing to that which remaineth to bee discouered, neither the soile, nor commodities. As we haue reason so to gather by the difference we found in our trauails: for although all which I haue before spoken of, haue bin discouered & experimented not far from the sea coast where was our abode & most of our trauailing: yet somtimes as we made our iourneies farther into the maine and countrey; we found the soyle to bee fatter; the trees greater and to growe thinner; the grounde more firme and deeper mould; more and larger champions; finer grasse and as good as euer we saw any in England; in some places rockie and farre more high and hillie ground; more plentie of their fruites; more abondance of beastes; the more inhabited with people, and of greater pollicie & larger dominions, with greater townes and houses.

Why may wee not then looke for in good hope from the inner parts of more and greater plentie, as well of other things, as of those which wee haue alreadie discouered? Vnto the Spaniardes happened the like in discouering the maine of the West Indies. The maine also of this countrey of *Virginia*, extending some wayes so many hundreds of leagues, as otherwise then by the relation of the inhabitants wee haue most certaine knowledge of, where yet no Christian Prince hath any possession or dealing, cannot but yeeld many kinds of excellent commodities, which we in our discouerie haue not yet seene.

What hope there is els to be gathered of the nature of the climate, being answerable to the Iland of *Iapan*, the land of *China, Persia, Iury*, the Ilandes of *Cyprus* and *Candy*, the South parts of *Greece, Italy*, and *Spaine*, and of many other notable and famous countreis, because I meane not to be tedious, I leaue to your owne consideration.

Whereby also the excellent temperature of the ayre there at all seasons, much warmer then in England, and neuer so violently hot, as sometimes is vnder & between the Tropikes, or nere them; cannot bee vnknowne vnto you without farther relation.

For the holsomnesse thereof I neede to say but thus much: that for all the want of prouision, as first of English victuall; excepting for twentie daies, wee liued only by drinking water and by the victuall of the countrey, of which some sorts were very straunge vnto vs, and might haue bene thought to haue altered our temperatures in such sort as to haue brought vs into some greeuous and dagerous diseases: secondly the wāt of English meanes, for the taking of beastes, fishe, and foule, which by the helpe only of the inhabitants and their meanes, coulde not bee so suddenly and eafily prouided for vs, nor in fo great numbers & quantities, nor of that choife as otherwife might haue bene to our better fatisfaction and contentment. Some want alfo wee had of clothes. Furthermore, in all our trauailes which were moft fpeciall and often in the time of winter, our lodging was in the open aire vpon the grounde. And yet I fay for all this, there were but foure of our whole company (being one hundred and eight) that died all the yeere and that but at the latter ende thereof and vpon none of the aforefaide caufes. For all foure efpecially three were feeble, weake, and fickly perfons before euer they came thither, and thofe that knewe them much marueyled that they liued fo long beeing in that cafe, or had aduentured to trauaile.

Seing therefore the ayre there is fo temperate and holfome, the foyle fo fertile and yeelding fuch commodities as I haue before mentioned, the voyage alfo thither to and fro beeing fufficiently experimented, to bee perfourmed thrife a yeere with eafe and at any feafon thereof : And the dealing of Sir *Water Raleigh* fo liberall in large giuing and graūting lande there, as is alreadie knowen, with many helpes and furtherances els : (The leaft that hee hath graunted hath beene fiue hundred acres to a man onely for the aduenture of his perfon:) I hope there remaine no caufe wherby the action fhould be mifliked.

If that thofe which fhall thiter trauaile to inhabite and plant bee but reafonably prouided for the firft yere as thofe are which were tranfported the laft, and beeing there doe vfe but that diligence and care as is requifite, and as they may with eefe : There is no doubt but for the time following they may haue victuals that is excellent good and plentie enough; fome more Englifhe fortes of cattaile alfo hereafter, as fome haue bene before, and are there yet remaining, may and fhall bee God willing thiter tranfported: So likewife our kinde of fruites, rootes, and hearbes may bee there planted and fowed, as fome haue bene alreadie, and proue wel: And in fhort time alfo they may raife of thofe fortes of commodities which I haue fpoken of as fhall both enrich them felues, as alfo others that fhall deale with them.

And this is all the fruites of our labours, that I haue thought neceffary to aduertife you of at this prefent: what els concerneth the nature and manners of the inhabitants of *Virginia*: The number with the particularities of the voyages thither made; and of the actions of fuch that haue bene by Sir *Water Raleigh* there in and there imployed, many worthy to bee remembred; as of the firft difcouerers of the Countrey: of our generall for the time Sir *Richard Greinuile*; and after his departure, of our Gouernour there Mafter *Rafe Lane*; with diuers other directed and imployed vnder theyr gouernement : Of the Captaynes and Mafters of the voyages made fince for tranfportation; of the Gouernour and affiftants of thofe alredie tranfported, as of many perfons, accidēts, and thinges els, I haue ready in a difcour-

feby

se by it self in maner of a Chronicle according to the course of times, and when time shall bee thought conuenient shall be also published.

Thus referring my relation to your fauourable constructions, expecting good successe of the action, from him which is to be acknowledged the authour and gouernour not only of this but of all things els, I take my leaue of you, this moneth of Februarii, 1 5 8 8.

F I N I S.

d 3

# THE TRVE PICTVRES
# AND FASHIONS OF
## THE PEOPLE IN THAT PAR-
## TE OF AMERICA NOVV CAL-
### LED VIRGINIA, DISCOWRED BY ENGLISMEN

sent thither in the years of our Lorde 1585. att the speciall charge and direction of
the Honourable SIR WALTER RALEGH Knigt Lord Warden
of the stannaries in the duchies of Corenwal and Oxford who
therin hath bynne fauored and auctorised by her
MAAIESTIE and her let-
ters patents.

*Translated out of Latin into English by*
*RICHARD HACKLVIT.*

*DILIGENTLYE COLLECTED AND DRAOW-*
*ne by IHON WHITE who was sent thiter speciallye and for thesame pur-*
*pose by the said SIR WALTER RALEGH the year abouesaid*
*1585. and also the year 1588. now cutt in copper andfirst*
*published by THEODORE de BRY att*
*his wone chardges.*

# THE TABLE
## OF ALL DE PICTV-
### RES CONTAINED IN
this Booke of Virginia.

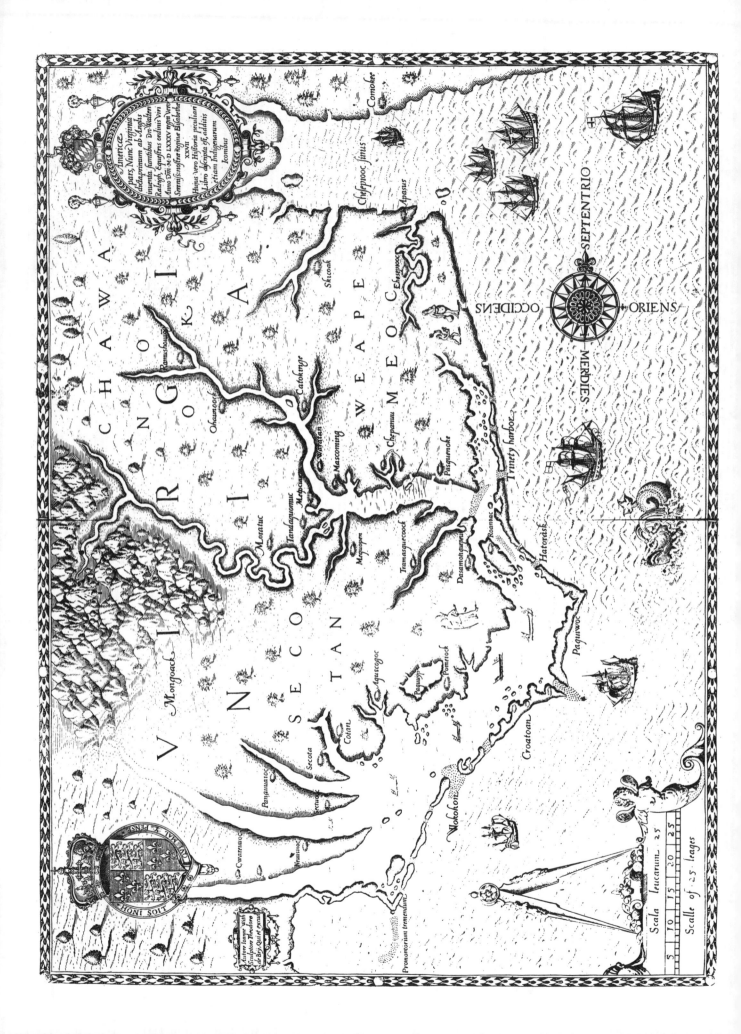

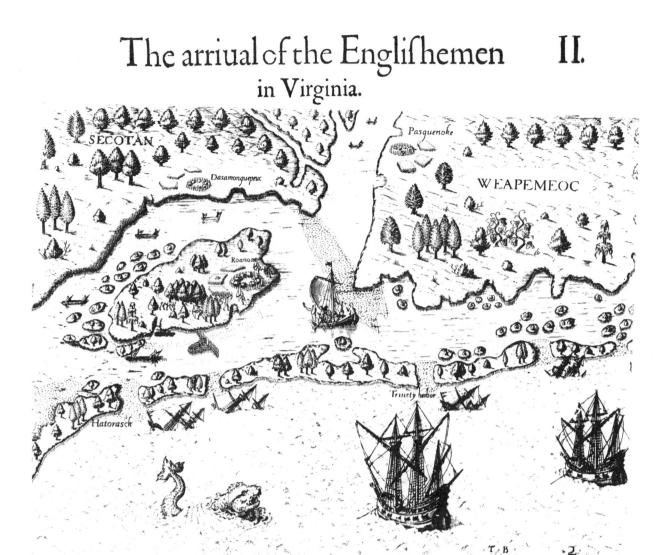

He sea coasts of Virginia arre full of Ilāds, wehr by the entrance into the mayne lād is hard to finde. For although they bee separated with diuers and sundrie large Diui-sion, which seeme to yeeld conuenient entrance, yet to our great perill we proued that they wear shallowe, and full of dangerous flatts, and could neuer perce opp into the mayne lād, vntill wee made trialls in many places with or small pinneß. At lengthe wee fownd an entrance vppon our mens diligent serche therof Affter that wee had passed opp, and sayled ther in for a short space we discouered a migthye riuer fallnige downe in to the sownde ouer againſt those Ilands, which neuerthelesse wee could not saile opp any thinge far by Reason of the shallewnes, the mouth ther of beinge annoyed with sands driuen in with the tyde therfore saylinge further, wee came vnto a Good bigg yland, the Inhabitante therof as soone as they saw vs began to make a great an horrible crye, as people which meuer befoer had seene men appa-relled like vs, and camme a way makinge out crys like w... i beasts or men out of their wyts. But been-ge gentlye called backe, wee offred the of our wares, as glasses, kniues, babies, and other trifles, which wee thougt they dcligted in. Soe they stood still, and perceuinge our Good will and courtesie came fawninge vppon vs, and bade us welcome. Then they brougt vs to their village in the iland called, Roanoac, and vnto their Weroans or Prince, which entertained vs with Reasonable curtesie, alt-houg the wear amased at the first sight of vs. Suche was our arriuall into the parte of the world, which we call Virginia, the stature of bodee of wich people, theyr attire, and maneer of lyuinge, their feasts, and banketts, I will particullerlye declare vnto yow.

He Princes of Virginia are attyred in ſuche manner as is expreſſed in this figure. They weare the haire of their heades long and bynde opp the ende of theſame in a knot vnder thier eares. Yet they cutt the topp of their heades from the forehead to the nape of the necke in manner of a cokſcombe, ſtirkinge a faier lóge pecher of ſome berd att the Begininge of the creſte vppun their foreheads, and another ſhort one on bothe ſeides about their eares. They hange at their eares ether thicke pearles, or ſomwhat els, as the clawe of ſome great birde, as cometh in to their fanſye. Moreouer They ether pownes, or paynt their forehead, cheeks, chynne, bodye, armes, and leggs, yet in another ſorte then the inhabitantz of Florida. They weare a chaine about their necks of pearles or beades of cop-per, wich they muche eſteeme, and ther of wear they alſo braſelets ohn their armes. Vnder their breſts about their bellyes appeir certayne ſpotts, whear they vſe to lett them ſelues bloode, when they are ſicke. They hange before thē the ſkinne of ſome beaſte verye feinelye dreſſet in ſuche ſorte, that the tayle hangeth downe behynde. They carye a quiuer made of ſmall ruſhes holding their bowe readie bent in on hand, and an arrowe in the other, radie to defend themſelues. In this manner they goe to warr, or tho their ſolemne feaſts and banquetts. They take muche pleaſure in huntinge of deer wher of theris great ſtore in the contrye, for yt is fruitfull, pleaſant, and full of Goodly woods. Yt hathe alſo ſtore of riuers full of diuers ſorts of fiſhe. When they go to battel they paynt their bo-dyes in the moſt terible manner that thei can deuiſe.

He woemé of Secotam are of Reasonable good proportion. In their goinge they carrye their hãds danglinge downe, and air dadil in a deer skinne verye excellétlye wel dressed, hanginge downe fró their nauell vnto the mydds of their thighes, which also couereth their hynder partz. The reste of their bodies are all bare. The forr parte of their haire is cutt shorte, the rest is not ouer Longe, thinne, and softe, and falling downe about their shoulders: They weare a Wrrath about their heads. Their foreheads, cheeks, chynne, armes and leggs are pownced. About their necks they wear a chaine, ether pricked or paynted. They haue small eyes, plaine and flatt noses, narrow foreheads, and broade mowths. For the most parte they hange at their eares chaynes of longe Pearles, and of some smootht bones. Yet their nayles are not longe, as the woemen of Florida. They are also deligtted with walkinge in to the fields, 'and besides the riuers, to see the huntinge of deers and catchinge of fische.

A  2

5

He Priests of the aforesaid Towne of Secota are well stricken in yeers, and as yt see-
meth of more experience then the comon sorte. They weare their heare cutt like a
creste, on the topps of thier heades as other doe, but the rest are cutt shorte, sauinge
those which growe aboue their foreheads in manner of a perriwigge. They also haue somwhat hanginge in their ears. They weare a shorte clocke made of fine hares
skinnes quilted with the hayre outwarde. The rest of thier bodie is naked.  They
are notable enchaunters, and for their pleasure they frequent the riuers, to kill with
their bowes, and catche wilde ducks, swannes, and
other fowles.

6           G · VEEN

Irgins of good parentage are apparelled altogether like the woemen of Secota aboue mentionned, sauing that they weare hanginge abowt their necks in steede of a chaine certaine thicke, and rownde pearles, with little beades of copper, or polished bones betweene them. They pounce their foreheads, cheeckes, armes and legs. Their haire is cutt with two ridges aboue their foreheads, the rest is trussed opp on a knott behinde, they haue broade mowthes, reasonable fair black eyes: they lay their hands often vppon their Shoulders, and couer their brests in token of maydenlike modestye. The rest of their bodyes are naked, as in the picture is to bee seene.
They deligt also in seeinge fishe taken in
the riuers.

A   4

He cheefe men of the yland and towne of Roanoac reace the haire of their crou-
nes of theyr heades cutt like a cokes cóbe, as thes other doe. The reft they wear lóge
as woemen and truſs them opp in a knott in the nape of their necks.  They hange
pearles ſtringe copper a threed att their eares, and weare bracelets on their armes of
pearles, or ſmall beades of copper or of ſmoothe bone called minſal, nether pain-
tinge nor powncings of them ſelues, but in token of authoritye, and honor, they wear a chaine of
great pearles, or copper beades or ſmoothe bones abowt their necks, and a plate of copper hinge v-
pon a ſtringe, from the nauel vnto the midds of their thighes. They couer themſelues before and be-
hynde as the woemé doe with a deers skynne handſomley dreſſed, and fringed, More ouer they fold
their armes together as they walke, or as they talke one wjth another in ſigne of wiſdome.
The yle of Roanoac is verye pleiſant, ond hath plaintie of fiſhe by reaſon of the Water that enuironeth theſame.

bout 20. milles from that Iland, neere the lake of Paquippe, ther is another towne called Pomeioock hard by the fea. The apparell of the cheefe ladyes of dat towne differeth but litle from the attyre of thofe which lyue in Roanaac. For they weare their haire truffed opp in a knott, as the maiden doe which we fpake of before, and haue their fkinnes pownced in thefame manner, yet they wear a chaine of great pearles, or beades of copper, or fmoothe bones 5. or 6. fold obout their necks, bearinge one arme in the fame, in the other hand they carye a gourde full of fome kinde of pleafant liquor. They tye deers fkinne doubled about them crochinge hygher about their breafts, which hange downe before almoft to their knees, and are almoft altogither naked behinde. Commonlye their yonge daugters of 7. or 8. yeares olde do waigt vpon them wearinge abowt them a girdle of fkinne, which hangeth downe behinde, and is drawen vnder neath betwene their twifte, and bownde aboue their nauel with mofe of trees betwene that and thier fkinnes to couer their priuiliers withall. After they be once paft 10. yeares of age, they wear deer fkinnes as the older forte do.
They are greatlye Diligted with puppetts, and babes which wear brought
oute of England.

# An ageed manne in his winter IX.
## garment.

He aged men of Pommeioocke are couered with a large skinne which is tyed vppon their shoulders on one side and hangeth downe beneath their knees wearinge their other arme naked out of the skinne, that they maye bee at more libertie. Those skynnes are Dressed with the hair on, and lyned with other furred skinnes. The yonnge men suffer noe hairr at all to growe vppon their faces but assoone as they growe they put them away, but when thy are come to yeeres they suffer them to growe although to say truthe they come opp verye thinne. They also weare their haire bownde op behynde, and, haue a creste on their heads like the others. The contrye abowt this plase is soe fruit full and good, that England is not to bee compared to yt.

**B**

I N the towne of Dasemonquepeuc distant from Roanoac 4. or 5. milles, the woemen are attired, and pownced, in suche sorte as the woemen of Roanoac are, yet they weare noe worathes vppon their heads, nether haue they their thighes painted with small pricks. They haue a strange manner of bearing their children, and quite contrarie to ours. For our woemen carrie their children in their armes before their brests, but they taking their sonne by the right hand, bear him on their backs, holdinge the left thighe in their lefte arme after a strange, and conuesnall fashion, as in the picture is to bee seene.

B 2

Hey haue comonlye coniurers or iuglers which vſe ſtrange geſtures, and often cō-
trarie to nature in their enchantments: For they be verye familiar with deuils, of
whome they enquier what their enemys doe, or other ſuche thinges. They ſhaue
all their heads ſauinge their creſte which they weare as other doe, and faſten a ſmall
black birde aboue one of their ears as a badge of their office. They weare nothinge
but a ſkinne which hangeth downe from their gyrdle, and couereth their priuityes. They weare a
bagg by their ſide as is expreſſed in the figure. The Inhabitants giue great credit vnto their ſpeeche, which oftentymes they finde
to bee true.

B 3

He manner of makinge their boates in Virginia is verye wonderfull. For wheras they want Inſtruments of yron , or other like vnto ours, yet they knowe howe to make them as handſomelye, to ſaile with whear they liſte in their Riuers, and to fiſhe with all, as ours. Firſt they chooſe ſome longe , and thicke tree, accordinge to the bignes of the boate which they would frame, and make a fyre on the grownd abowt the Roote therof, kindlinge the ſame by little , and little with drie moſſe of trees, and chipps of woode that the flame ſhould not mounte opp to highe, and burne to muche of the lengte of the tree· When yt is almoſt burnt thorough, and readye to fall they make a new fyre, which they ſuffer to burne vntill the tree fall of yt owne accord. Then burninge of the topp, and bowghs of the tree in ſuche wyſe that the bodie of theſame may Retayne his iuſt lengthe, they raiſe yt vppon potes laid ouer croſſ wiſe vppon forked poſts, at ſuche a reaſonable heighte as rhey may handſomlye worke vp-pó yt. Then take they of the barke with certayne ſhells: thy reſerue the, innermoſt parte of the lenn-ke , for the nethermoſt parte of the boate. On the other ſide they make a fyre according to the lengthe of the bodye of the tree, ſauinge at both the endes. That which they thinke is ſufficientlye burned they quenche and ſcrape away with ſhells, and makinge a new fyre they burne yt agayne, and ſoe they continne ſomtymes burninge and ſometymes ſcrapinge, vntill the boate haue ſufficient bothowmes. This god indueth thiſe ſauage people with ſufficient reaſon to make thinges neceſſarie to ſerue their turnes.

# XIII.

## Their manner of fishynge in
## Virginia.

Hey haue likewife a notable way to catche fishe in their Riuers. for whear as they lacke both yron, and fteele, they fafte vnto their Reedes or longe Rodds, the hollowe tayle of a certaine fishe like to a sea crabb in fteede of a poynte, wehr with by nighte or day they ftricke fishes, and take them opp into their boates. They alfo know how to vfe the prickles, and pricks of other fishes. They alfo make weares, with fettinge opp reedes or twigges in the water, which they foe plant one within a nother, that they growe ftill narrower, and narrower, as appeareth by this figure. Ther was neuer feene amonge vs foe cunninge a way to take fish withall, wherof fondrie fortes as they fownde in their Riuers vnlike vnto ours. which are alfo of a verye good tafte. Dowbtlefs yt is a pleafant fighte to fee the people, fomtymes wadinge, and goinge fomtymes failinge in thofe Riuers, which are shallowe and not deepe, free from all care of heapinge opp Riches for their pofterite, content with their ftate, and liuinge frendlye together of thofe thinges which god of his bountye hath giuen vnto them, yet without giuinge hym any thankes according to his defarte.

So fauage is this people, and depriued of the true knowledge of god.

For they haue none other then is mentionned before in this worke.

Fter they haue taken ftore of fifhe, they gett them vnto a place fitt to drefs yt. Ther they fticke vpp in the grownde 4. ftakes in a fquare roome, and lay 4 potes vppon them, and others ouer thwart thefame like vnto an hurdle, of fufficient heigthe. and layinge their fifhe vppon this hurdle, they make a fyre vnderneathe to broile the fame, not after the manner of the people of Florida, which doe but fchorte, and harden their meate in the fmoke onlye to Referue thefame duringe all the winter. For this people referuinge nothing for ftore, thei do broile, and fpend away all att once and when they haue further neede, they rofte or feethe frefh, as wee fhall fee heraffter. And when as the hurdle can not holde all the fifhes, they hange the Reft by the fyrres on fticks fett vpp in the grounde a gainft the fyre, and than they finifhe the reft of their cookerye. They take good heede that they bee not burntt. When the firft are broyled they lay others on, that weare newlye broughte, continuinge the dreffinge of their meate in this forte, vntill they thincke they haue fufficient.

· G · VEEN

Heir woemen know how to make earthen veſſells with ſpecial Cunninge and that
ſo large and fine, that our potters with lhoye wheles can make noe better: ant then
Remoue them from place to place as eaſelye as we candoe our braſſen kettles. After they haue ſet them vppon an heape of erthe to ſtay them from fallinge, they
putt wood vnder which being kyndled one of them taketh great care that the fyre
burne equallye Rounde abowt. They or their woemen fill the veſſel with water,
and then putt they in fruite, fleſh, and fiſh, and lett all boyle together like a galliemaufrye, which
the Spaniarde call, olla podrida. Then they putte yt out into diſches, and ſett before the com-
panye, and then they make good cheere together. Yet are they moderate in their eatinge wher
by they auoide ſicknes. I would to god wee would followe their exemple. For wee ſhould bee
free from many kynes of diſeaſyes which wee fall into by ſumptwous and vnſeaſonable banketts,
continuallye deuiſinge new ſawces, and prouocation of gluttonnye to ſatiſſie
our vnſatiable appetite.

Heir manner of feeding is in this wife. They lay a matt made of bents one the grownde and fett their meate on the mids therof, and then fit downe Rownde, the men vppon one fide, and the woemen on the other. Their meate is Mayz fodden, in fuche forte as I defcribed yt in the former treatife of verye good tafte, deers flefche, or of fome other beafte, and fifhe. They are verye fober in their eatinge, and trinkinge, and confequentlye verye longe liued becaufe they doe not opprefs nature.

C

# XVII.

# Their manner of prainge vvith Rat-
tels abowt te fyer.

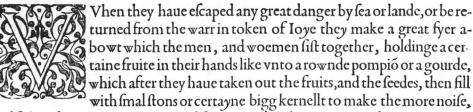Vhen they haue escaped any great danger by sea or lande, or be returned from the warr in token of Ioye they make a great fyer abowt which the men, and woemen sist together, holdinge a certaine fruite in their hands like vnto a rownde pompió or a gourde, which after they haue taken out the fruits, and the seedes, then fill with smal stons or certayne bigg kernellt to make the more noise, and fasten that vppon a sticke, and singinge after their manner, they make merrie: as my selfe obserued and noted downe at my beinge amonge them. For it is a strange custome, and worth the obseruation.

# XVIII.

## Theirdanſes vvhich they vſe att their hyghe feaſtes.

T a Certayne tyme of the yere they make a great, and ſolemne feaſte wherunto their neighbours of the townes adioninge repayre from all parts, euery man attyred in the moſt ſtrange faſhion they can deuiſe hauinge certayne marks on the backs to declare of what place they bee. The place where they meet is a broade playne, abowt the which are planted in the grownde certayne poſts carued with heads like to the faces of Nonnes couered with theyr vayles. Then beeing ſett in order they dance, ſinge, and vſe the ſtrangeſt geſtures that they can poſſiblye deuiſe. Three of the fayreſt Virgins, of the companie are in the mydds, which imbraſſinge one another doe as yt wear turne abowt in their dancinge. All this is donne after the ſunne is ſett for auoydinge of heate. When they are weerye of dancinge. they goe oute of the circle, and come in vntill their dances be ended, and they goe to make merrye as is expreſſed in the 16. figure.

# XIX.

## The Tovvne of Pomeiooc.

He townes of this contrie are in a maner like vnto those which are in Florida , yet are they not soe stronge nor yet preserüed with soe great care. They are compassed abowt with poles starcke faste in the grownd, but they are not verye stronge. The entrance is verye narrowe as may be seene by this picture, which is made accordinge to the forme of the towne of Pomeiooc. Ther are but few howses therin, saue those which belonge to the kinge and his nobles. On the one side is their tempel separated from the other howses, and marked with the letter A. yt is builded rownde, and couered with skynne matts, and as yt wear compassed abowt. With cortynes without windowes, and hath noe ligthe but by the doore. On the other side is the kings lodginge marked with the letter B. Their dwellinges are builded with certaine potes fastened together , and couered with matts which they turne op as high as they thinke good, and soe receue in the lighte and other. Some are also couered with boughes of trees, as euery man lusteth or liketh best. They keepe their feasts and make good cheer together in the midds of the towne as yt is described in they 17. Figure. When the towne standeth fare from the water they digg a great poude noted with the letter C. wherhence they fetche as muche water as they neede.

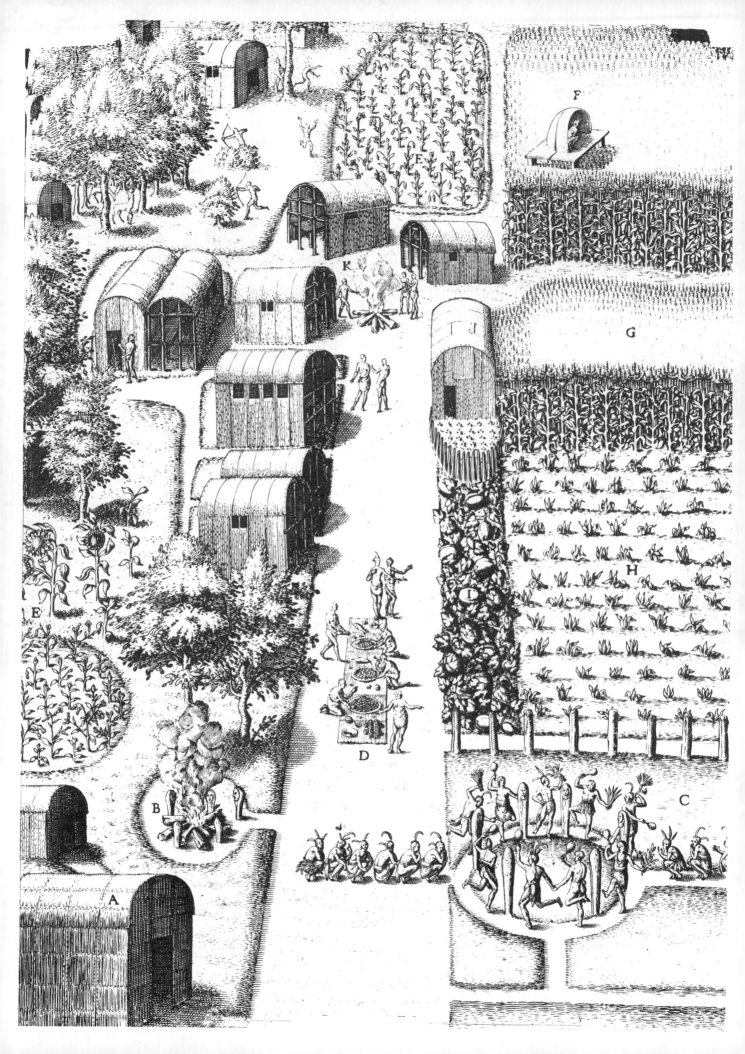

# X X.

# The Tovvne of Secota.

Heir townes that are not inclosed with poles aire common-lye fayrer. Then suche as are inclosed, as appereth in this fi-gure which liuelye expresseth the towne of Secotam. For the howses are Scattered heer and ther, and they haue garde-in expressed by the letter E. wherin groweth Tobacco which the inhabitants call Vppowoc. They haue also groaues whe-rin thei take deer, and fields vherin they sowe their corne. In their corne fields they builde as yt weare a scaffolde wher on they sett a cottage like to a rownde chaire, signiffied by F. wherin they place one to watche. for there are suche nomber of fowles, and beasts, that vnless they keepe the better wat-che, they would soone deuoure all their corne. For which cause the wat-cheman maketh continual cryes and noyse. They sowe their corne with a certaine distance noted by H. other wise one stalke would choke the growthe of another and the corne would not come vnto his rypeurs G. For the leaues therof are large, like vnto the leaues of great reedes. They haue also a seuerall broade plotte C. whear they meete with their neighbours, to celebrate their cheefe solemne feastes as the 18. picture doth declare: and a place D. whear af-ter they haue ended their feaste they make merrie togither. Ouer against this place they haue a rownd plott B. wher they assemble themselues to make their solemne prayers. Not far from which place ther is a lardge buil-dinge A. wherin are the tombes of their kings and princes, as will appere by the 22. figure likewise they haue garden notted bey the letter I. wherin they vse to sowe pompions. Also a place marked with K. wherin the make a fyre att their solemne feasts, and hard without the towne a riuer L. from whence they fetche their water. This people therfore voyde of all couetousnes lyue cherfullye and att their harts ease. Butt they solemnise their feasts in the nigt, and therfore they keepe verye great fyres to auoyde darkenes, ant to testifie their Ioye.

21

 He people of this cuntrie haue an Idol, which they call K I W A S A : yt is carued of woode in lengthe 4. foote whofe heade is like the heades of the people of Florida, the face is of a flesh colour, the breft white, the reft is all blacke, the thighes are alfo fpottet with whitte. He hath a chayne abowt his necke of white beades, betweene which are other Rownde beades of copper which they efteeme more then golde or filuer. This Idol is placed in the temple of the towne of Secotam, as the keper of the kings dead corpfes. Somtyme they haue two of thes idoles in theyr churches, and fomtine 3. but neuer aboue, which they place in a darke corner wher they fhew tetrible. Thes poore foules haue none other knowledge of god although I thinke them verye Defirous to know the truthe. For when as wee kneeled downe on our knees to make our prayers vnto god, they went abowt to imitate vs, and when they faw we moued our lipps, they alfo dyd the like. Wherfore that is verye like that they might eafelye be brongt to the knowledge of the gofpel. God of his mercie grant them this grace.

D    2

# XXII.

# The Tombe of their Werovvans or Cheiff Lordes.

He builde a Scaffolde 9. or 10. foote hihe as is expreſſed in this figure vnder the tōbs of theit Weroans, or cheeſe lordes which they couer with matts, and lai the dead corpſes of their weroans theruppon in manner followinge. firſt the bowells are taken forthe. Then layinge downe the ſkinne, they cutt all the fleſh cleane from the bones, which the drye in the ſonne, and well dryed the incloſe in Matts, and place at their feete. Then their bones (remaininge ſtill faſtened together with the ligaments whole and vncorrupted) are couered a gayne with leather, and their carcaſe faſhioned as yf their fleſh wear not taken away. They lapp eache corps in his owne ſkinne after theſame in thus handled, and lay yt in his order by the corpſes of the other cheeſ lordes. By the dead bodies they ſett their Idol Kiwaſa, wher of we ſpake in the former chapiter : For they are perſuaded that theſame doth kepe the dead bodyes of their cheeſe lordes that nothinge may hurt them. Moreouer vnder the foreſaid ſcaffolde ſome on of their preiſts hath his lodginge, which Mumbleth his prayers nighte and day, and hath charge of the corpſes. For his bedd he hath two deares ſkinnes ſpredd on the grownde, yf the wether bee cold hee maketh a fyre to warme by withall. Thes poore ſoules are thus inſtructed by natute to reuerence their princes euen after their death.

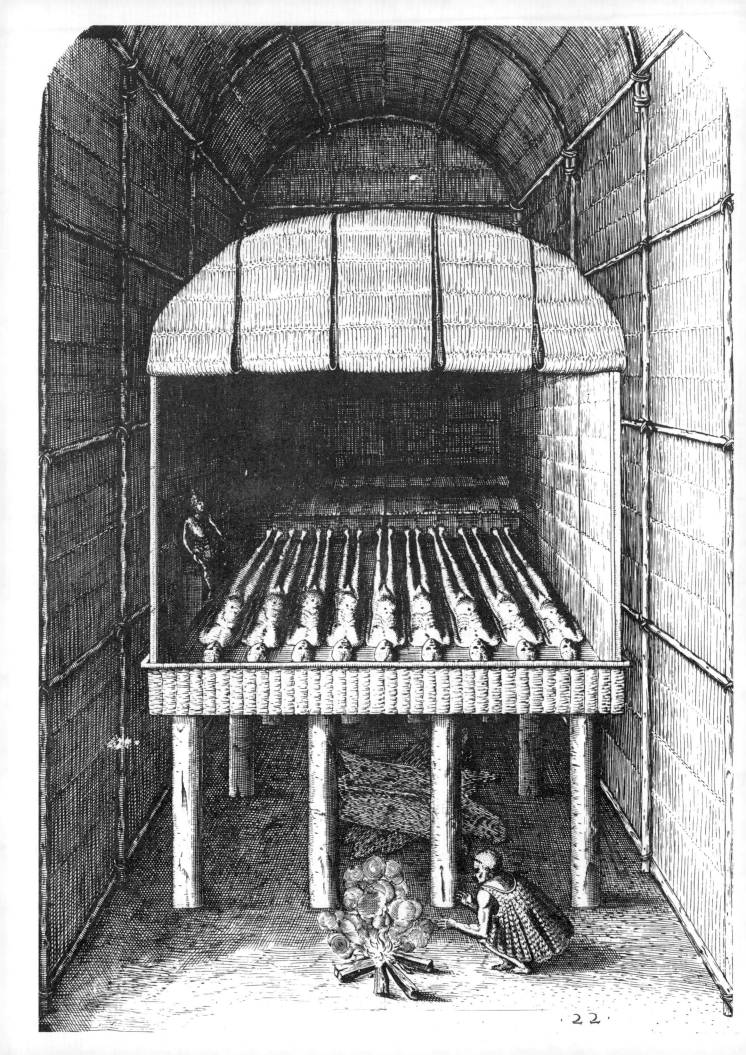

22

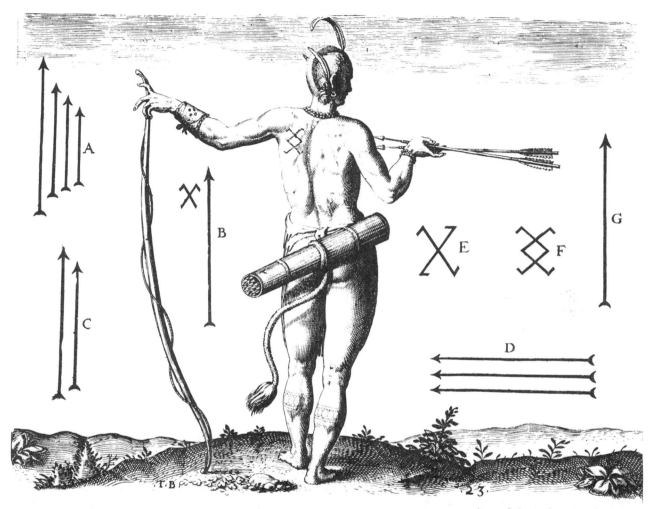

He inhabitāts of all the cuntrie for the most parte haue marks rased on their backs, wherby yt may be knowen what Princes subiects they bee, or of what place they haue their originall. For which cause we haue set downe those marks in this figure, and haue annexed the names of the places, that they might more easelye be discerned. Which industrie hath god indued them withal although they be verye sinple, and rude. And to confesse a truthe I cannot remember, that euer I saw a better or quietter people then they.

The marks which I obserued amonge them, are heere put downe in order folowinge.

The marke which is expressed by A. belongeth tho Wingino, the cheefe lorde of Roanoac.

That which hath B. is the marke of Wingino his sisters husbande.

Those which be noted with the letters, of C. and D. belonge vnto diverse chefe lordes in Secotam.

Those which haue the letters E. F. G. are certaine cheefe men of Pomeiooc, and Aquascogoc.

# A TABLE
# OF THE PRINCI-
## PALL THINGES THAT
are contained in this Historie, after the
order of the Alphabet.

F 3

# The Table.

Turkie

# The Table.

F I N I S.

*Faults escaped in the impression. the first nombre signiffie the*
*page, the second the Linne.*

Pag.11.lin.22 reade, and. pag.14.lin.14. reade sodden. lin.27. reade, about. pag.
16.lin.19. reade, sacrifice. pag.20.lin.18. reade Discouery. pag.23.li 3. reade hatchets.
In the preface of the figures lin.17. reade lyuely. lin.23. reade late. figure 2.lin.1.
reade wher. lin.7. reade fallinge. lin.10. reade neuer. 18. bodye.
Fig.3.lin.5. reade vppon fig.7 lin.11. reade and, fig.8.lin.2. reade that. fig.12.lin.
11. reade they. lin.16. reade scrapinge. fig.13.lin. 10. reade also. fig.16.lin.6. drinkinge.
fig 21.lin.12. about.
The rest if any be the discreete reader may easily amend.

# SOM PICTVRE,
# OF THE PICTES
## WHICH IN THE OLDE
tyme dyd habite one part of the
great Bretainne.

THE PAINTER OF WHOM I HAVE
had the firſt of the Inhabitans of Virginia, giue my allſo thees 5. Figures
fallowinge, fownd as hy did aſſured my in a oolld Engliſh cronicle, the which
I wold well ſett to the ende of thees firſt Figures, for to ſhowe how that
the Inhabitants of the great Bretannie haue bin in ti-
mes paſt as ſauuage as thoſe of
Virginia.

# The trvve picture of one
## Picte I.

IN tymes paſt the Pictes, habitans of one part of great Bretainne, which is nowe nammed England, wear ſauuages, and did paint all their bodye after the maner followinge. the did lett their haire growe as fare as their Shoulders, ſauinge thoſe which hange vppon their forehead, the which the did cutt. They ſhaue all their berde except the muſtaches, vppon their breaſt wear painted the head of ſom birde, ant about the pappes as yt waere beames of the ſune, vppon the bellye ſum feere full and monſtreus face, ſpreedinge the beames verye fare vppon the thighes. Vppon the tow knees ſom faces of lion, and vppon their leggs as yt hath been ſhelles of fiſh. Vppon their Shoulders griffones heades, and then they hath ſerpents abowt their armes: They caried abowt their necks one ayerne ringe, and another abowt the midds of their bodye, abowt the bellye, and the ſaids hange on a chaine, a cimeterre or turkie ſoorde, the did carye in one arme a target made of wode, and in the other hande a picke, of which the ayerne was after the manner of a Lick, whith taſſels on, and the other ende with a Rounde boule. And when they hath ouercomme ſome of their ennemis, they did neuer felle to carye a we their heads with them.

T·B·J·

TB 2

# The trvve picture of a vvomen
## Picte II.

He woemen of the pictes aboue said wear noe worser for the warres then the men. And wear paynted after the manner followinge, hauinge their heads bear, did lett their hairre flyinge. abowt their Showlders wear painted with griffon heades, the lowe parts and thighes with lion faces, or some other beaste as yt commeth best into their fansye, their brest hath a maner of a half moone, with a great stare, and fowre lesser in booth the sides, their pappes painted in maner of beames of the sonne, and amóg all this a great litteninge starre vppon their brests. The saids of som pointes or beames, and the hoolle bellye as a sonne, the armes, thighes, and leggs well painted, of diuerses Figures : The dyd also carye abowt theyr necks an ayern Ringe, as the men did, and suche a girdle with the soorde hainginge, hauinge a Picke or a lance in one hande, and twoe dardz in the other.

# The trvve picture of a yonge
## dowgter of the Pictes I I I.

He yong dougters of the pictes, did alſo lett their haire flyinge and wear alſo painted ouer all the body, ſo much that noe mer could not faynde any different, yf the hath not vſe of another faſhion of paintinge, for the did paint themſelues of ſondrye kinds of flours, and of the faireſt that they cowld feynde. being fourniſhed for the reſt of ſuch kinds of weappon as the woemen wear as you may ſee by this preſent picture a thinge trwelly worthie of admiration.

TB 3